CONTENTS

PREFACE INTRODUCING A STRONG NEW GLOBAL BRITAIN	2
1. INTRODUCTION	6
2. THE NEED FOR BOLD THOUGHT AND ACTION	10
3. TOP-DOWN POST-BREXIT UK FOREIGN POLICY	13
4. UK DEFENCE FORCE STRUCTURING	20
5. THE RIGHT EXPENDITURE LEVELS VERSUS THE RISKS WE FACE	34
6. THE IMPLEMENTATION PROCESS	36
7. CONCLUSION: TO BE OR NOT TO BE	40

PREFACE
INTRODUCING A STRONG NEW GLOBAL BRITAIN

Today Britain is living through a time of crisis, triggered by the coronavirus pandemic and the consequent economic contraction. To compound the uncertainties ahead, Britain is also in the final stage of its Brexit process. However, every signal from the five-stage roadmap model indicates that stage is in reality a time of great opportunity for Britain to reset and rebuild as we return to our global maritime heritage and increase our integration into a global trading system in a new multi-polar world. A time when the contraction of American power will create numerous power vacuums that Britain can move into (for example, the funding of the WHO), to shore up the democratic world against the rising threats of dictatorships. Although spending may apparently be constrained when viewed with the traditional thinking of cost and no benefit, increased defence spending in reality will provide both greater security and a major boost to the British economy through multiple benefits.

Conversely, whilst opportunities abound in the post-Brexit world, it is also a time of great risk if we continue our wilful blindness to the threats from Russia and China, and fail to rapidly increase the defence and power projections capabilities by a significant measure.

This publication is a sincere effort to capture the national imperative and offer a fresh and uninhibited view, based on strategic analysis and historical extractions, which will allow a post-Brexit Britain to reset with a global perspective. This view is based on the options available to support such a Defence expansion, driven by significant defence and security investment and accompanied by new global thought processes and enhanced leadership.

The origins of this publication date back to the disastrous government review of 2015 where it was clear that both our political and military leaders had lost their way following years of cost-cutting and wilful blindness to rising threats. The combination of a body politic with minimal military experience or strategic vision combined with a highly politicised peacetime military leadership has proven disastrous for the security of the nation. Today Britain desperately needs to shift its mindset from one of cost-cutting to one of rearmament, accompanied by a new powerful military-industrial complex, to counter the increasingly volatile geopolitical environment in which we now find ourselves.

Today, in a similar process to the distraction provided by Islamic terrorism, we face the risk of being distracted by the current pandemic away from the single greatest risk that Britain faces this decade – the aggressive rise of China and its hegemonic challenge to America and the West, compounded by the threat of an opportunist Russia.

Although most of the human population would passionately condemn it, war has sadly always been a defining characteristic of human existence. The hard reality is that wars are a Darwinist process that remove the old and weak empires and nations and replace them with stronger, younger systems. Thus history has been driven by the cycles described in the five-stage roadmap, in which, as nations expanded, resource competition with neighbours was created. Then, as polarisation intensified, war followed. Thus war is the point at which collective resource competition gives way to conflict. Today we are once more approaching such a critical point in the commodity cycle, an imminent price peak in 2025-27 that will trigger a war of Chinese expansion, unless strongly deterred by the West.

Expanding empires and nations will only make a challenge if they perceive that their potential opponent is weakening and in decline. Thus, in such a predatory attack, the relative power between two nations or empires is critical to war being deterred or starting. As the balance of power shifts towards the younger, expanding system, the risks of conflict increase dramatically. This occurs because of the expansionary drive of the challenger (China), but the trigger for war is always a perceived sign of weakness in the established hegemonic power (America and the West).

Some might well argue that Britain's forces compared to those of China and Russia might be considered small and insignificant, asking the question, can we make a difference? But the real question should be, can we afford not to make a difference? As described in the book *Lions Led By Lions*, the British Expeditionary Force deployed in France failed to be of a size to deter Germany's attack, a political failure that Britain should never make again. However, Britain did perform exceptionally well in 1914, saving France from defeat, and again in 1918, after a massive wave of military innovation that invented and deployed a new form of combined arms warfare, Britain and the Allies went on to win the war on the Western Front. Furthermore, by following the lead of the Australians, who are now building a navy of considerable size to protect against China, Britain can in turn lead by example to encourage other European allies to follow a similar path to greater collective security.

As Chamberlain and Roosevelt found to their cost in the run up to WWII, hope and appeasement are guaranteed paths to conflict. Indeed, even Stalin fell into this trap with his non-aggression pact with Hitler, during which for two years he exported grains and critical resources that strengthened Nazi Germany's war effort, and weakened the Russian position. Conversely, as the Cold War proved, full spectrum deterrence really does work as effectively between great nations, as it does on the playing field against a bully.

History provides us with powerful and useful lessons when it drawn from the five-stage roadmap. In the 1930s, the RAF held the belief that a bomber would always reach its target. This concept was encouraged by the RAF to ensure its differentiation from tactical air power and avoid any risk of future control by the Army. It was only through public awareness of the German threat that Fighter Command was created in time to defend England and win the Battle of Britain. Echoing the past, in Downing Street today there are numerous senior members of government who are deluded enough to argue that the age of kinetic weapons has given way to the dominance of cyber warfare. This mindset is as dangerous to the nation's security as the idea in the

1930s that a bomber would always get through. To avoid falling into such a major pitfall, awareness must be raised within both the public and the government that cyber security is but one component of a full-spectrum defensive capability. Thus kinetic weaponry must receive our attention as the former does not replace the latter. Rather, it works in tandem, supporting and reinforcing where necessary.

With this in mind, this *Global Forecaster UK Strategic Defence Review 2020* seeks to redefine what Britain should be doing both to maximise its economic expansion and simultaneously deter Chinese and Russian aggression. With the lead time to produce new weapon systems being measured in years, this 2020 Defence Review is the Now or Never moment for Britain.

Below: A soldier from 3 PARA Battle Group during Exercise Askari Storm; demonstrating bold intent. *Credit: UK MoD © Crown copyright 2020*

1.0 INTRODUCTION

1.1 RISING THREATS

There are times in history where threats remain latent and multiple scenario planning is applicable. However, today, based on Global Forecaster's models, two very major threats represent a clear and present danger to Britain's national security. These first degree threats currently dwarf all others and require the nation's immediate attention. These threats are Russia and China.

Russia and China have manifested as threats not just because of their internal expansionary drivers, but because of the long-term decline in Western power that has created a vacuum of opportunity. Those in Europe who question the threat of Chinese military expansion should be asking the questions: 'Why is Australia modernising its defence capabilities with a focus on China?' and 'Why is the United States Navy reconfiguring 60% of its capability to contain Chinese expansion?'.

1.2 AMERICA, THE TIRED HEGEMONY

There is no doubt that America is finding the role of global policeman exhausting, with its debt burden. With increasingly limited resources, it will be forced to focus on the primary threat of China and withdraw forces from Europe, which will give Putin greater leverage to threaten Europe. Meanwhile, irrespective of who is the next president, America will inevitably demand, quite rightly, that Britain takes more responsibility for its own defence. Thus, the clear message to Britain is that we cannot rely on America to continue to defend our national interests by supporting our systematic military weakness.

1.3 POST-BREXIT BRITAIN

Based on the Cycle of Empires in *Breaking the Code of History*, Britain has completed its new phase of regionalisation as marked by Brexit. This manifestation of new national energy and identity has been echoed in Britain's sporting success in the 2012 Olympics and other fields. However, atypical of the cycle is that Britain has not maintained and enhanced its British defence capabilities to be commensurate with its new Brexit path back to a global maritime nation.

1.4 HISTORY REPEATING ITSELF

Many would argue that the world today is different from the past as communication is so advanced and the world has never been so globalised. However, this was also a common argument prior to the outbreak of WW1. What really matters is that the basic behavioural patterns of expansive nations have not changed. This has been explicitly demonstrated by China's behaviour over the last decade and by the regional civil war in the Middle East. These two evolutions have taken place despite the increased process of globalisation and recent unprecedented levels of communication.

To compound this unrecognised threat, there is a general impression in Downing Street that large scale conventional warfare is a thing of the past. However, only the foolish would believe that an aggressively expansive nation would not use all means at its disposal to control the globe. While cyber warfare capabilities might add a new dimension to such a conflict, they will always be but one element in a multi-strand war fighting capability. Most critically, cyber warfare is a vital component of intelligence gathering that has powerful applications against network-centric warfare.

Opposite: The People's Liberation Army and Navy (PLA & PLAN) has undergone a rapid modernisation and consequent increased offensive capability, clearly and regularly exhorted by their Commander, President Xi, to be ready for war.
Credit: Shutterstock

Opposite, top: HMS *Defender* using her Sea Viper air missile defence system. Whilst currently a world leading air defence destroyer, the Type 45 needs to be upgraded to counter ballistic missile threats by radar and system upgrades and the integration of Mark 41 launches able to fire the US SM6 anti-ballistic missiles (ABMs). Additionally more ABM-capable Type 45s will have to be built, as with the advent of Chinese DF21 and DF26 missiles in future both warships and merchant ships will be vulnerable to long-range attack.
Credit: UK MoD © Crown copyright 2020

Below: UK F-35B Lightning fighter launching from HMS *Queen Elizabeth*. The melding of the F35B and UK strike carriers provides two strategic assets that can project power anywhere in the world and keep vital sea lanes open and ensure that threats are kept further away from Britain's shores.
Credit: UK MoD © Crown copyright 2019

Furthermore, in peer-to-peer wars of expansion, when the first levels of high-tech weaponry have been deployed and destroyed, the conflict quickly becomes an additional war. In this situation, reserve weapons of lower sophistication are then deployed and the winner will be the side with the greatest depth of resources at the highest relative levels of sophistication.

1.5 HOW MUCH SHOULD THE UK BE SPENDING ON DEFENCE?

A major question is what we can afford to spend on defence? The immediate counter-question is can we afford not to with the current threats on the horizon? The reality is that quantitative easing, otherwise known as the printing of money, has failed to compensate for the weakness in Western economies. The only substitute will be a new version of direct investment similar to America's New Deal during the 1930s. The natural place for this to start will be government investment in the UK's military-industrial complex and defence. That will build capacity and create jobs. It will also reduce the unit costs of defence items as greater numbers of units are built, bringing significant cost benefits. Additionally, in the era of Brexit, a strong defence capability will be needed to secure our resource chains and will be a significant bargaining chip in trade deals with nations threatened by China or Russia as they seek to strengthen alliances.

1.6 THE NEED FOR A BOLD AND STRONG BRITAIN TO MAXIMISE BREXIT

With these key threat drivers and the added impetus that Britain has left the EU to once more stand alone as a sovereign nation, it is time for a bold change as once made by the Parliamentarians of England during and after the Civil War. In pursuing this change, we must create a new model of defence policy that will protect and expand the nation in the challenging times ahead. Today, in a time when weapons systems are vastly more complex and take years longer to build than their counterparts in 1940, we are falling into the same trap as our ancestors. To send any of our airmen or sailors into war without stealth systems to give them camouflage and a chance of survival would be the equivalent of sending airmen in 1940 to war i n a Fairly Battle or Swordfish. It would be careless and irresponsible.

Unless we act now to change our defence policies and dramatically increase our spending on defence, in all probability it will be third time unlucky for Britain and we will lose the next major war, possibly before it even starts. The timing of the greatest risk of impeding conflict will be from 2025 onward for two reasons. First, due to the anticipated peak of the next commodity cycle. And second, because of the new five-year plan that China is implementing to build an internally fuelled consumer society bolstered by a militarised economy. Thus, to deter a future conflict, Britain must have implemented its defence reforms within five years. This is effectively a war timeline which will require radical reforms of the Ministry of Defence (MoD), combined with new rapid design, manufacturing and deployment protocols.

This 2020 Defence Review could well decide the very existence of Britain as a nation.

2.0 THE NEED FOR BOLD THOUGHT AND ACTION

2.1 A CRITICAL POINT IN BRITAIN'S HISTORY

The 2015 Strategic Defence Review was disastrous from the very moment it was published, primarily because it failed to anticipate today's threat environment and the trends in new weapons and forces deployed by Russia and China whilst at the same time running the UK forces down to the point of ineffectiveness.

Five years on, the government's lukewarm approach to defence feels like Groundhog Day. This is despite the major changes in the global geopolitical threat landscape. Now, the 2020 Review is without doubt the most important Defence Review in decades. One that I fear will decide the very survival of this island nation.

2.2 THE SCOPE OF THE REVIEW

Today, the Integrated Review of Security, Defence, Development and Foreign Policy is known as the Integrated Review. It differs from previous reviews as it will start from the top down with a foreign policy review rather than from the bottom up as in the past. Boris Johnson summarised the review's laudable objectives as follows:

1. **Foreign policy**: To define the United Kingdom's role in the world as well as its long-term strategic aims for national security and foreign policy. Additionally, address the risks and threats Britain faces and deduce how the UK can strengthen its relationships with allies.

2. **Force structuring**: To determine the military capabilities required for the next decade and beyond to pursue the UK's objectives.

3. **Institutional reforms**: Across the Defence and Security sector, for the MoD, the armed forces and the industrial military complex to achieve the above goals.

4. **The implementation process and progress evaluation**: Although not included by Boris, I would include the budget allocation in this section.

2.3 CONCERNS FOR THE OUTCOME OF THIS REVIEW

However, the 2020 review comes after two decades of cutting our military capability to the point of ineffectiveness. Simultaneously, we face the greatest military threat since the Cold War. These threats from both China and Russia have been copiously detailed in previous Global Forecaster Updates. The consequence is that just as Britain is stepping out into the world once more as an independent maritime nation it is facing very significant global threats to its supply lines, homeland and democratic values. If these threats continue to grow at their current rate they will inevitably threaten the nation's very integrity and continuance.

Much as this review appears to be different on the surface, I fear, along with many observers, that the outcome will be the same because our political leaders fail to appreciate:

1. **The lessons of the Cold War**. The Cold War remained cold through a commitment to deterrence across the full spectrum of warfare that allowed no gaps from which the USSR could gain leverage.

2. **The aggressive intentions of Russia and China** that could result in war if not deterred with a broad spectrum capability.

3. **Revolutions in military affairs**: The significant instability to the current balance of power that new weapons systems will induce will allow China and Russia to close the capability gap, with a serious danger of them even overtaking the West.

4. **Wars are catastrophic events**: Whilst arms races and deterrence are both expensive, the price of war is catastrophic.

5. **Accelerated economic growth**. Increased defence investment could fuel an expansion in Britain's industrial-military complex which could be a source of jobs and national revenue as well as the basis of strong global commercial alliances.

6. **The Army could educate the unemployed** if it were to be split into a new high-tech modern combat force and simultaneously operate a national training and development programme for the young, who would otherwise be unemployed.

2.4 SAME PLAN, SAME OUTCOME

Meanwhile, the Defence Chiefs of Staff (COS) are acting out the same game-plan as in past reviews, hoping for a different outcome. The outcome will only change once they understand the losing game that they have been playing for two decades. It is one based on the MoD creating a budget that drives each service to fight each other for money for their favourite programme. The net result is that the loser is Britain, the nation the COS are meant to be protecting. The situation is very similar to the Chin nation (as Northern China was once known) encouraging the Mongol tribes to fight each other. The arrival of Genghis Khan changed all of that as he united the tribes to a common cause and then subjugated the Chin. There is a great lesson to be learned from that. **The current negative loop can best be described as follows.**

The COS have two principal responsibilities: deliver fighting efficiency: and maintain morale. The former drives them to short-term operational delivery, at the expense of longer-term programmes, and the latter drives them to deliver professionally satisfying operational activity and support, when resources for both are in short supply. So, the COS are, very largely, hostages to the limitation in resources. Whilst their aspiration is to create resource headroom to transform, they cannot. And, arguably, though ministers want transformation, they too are locked in a 'deliver today or die' political space, in a world governed by platform counting, while fighting with the Treasury to minimise further cuts. Thus, only extra resources will unlock this negative loop. The only option is for the COS to start thinking outside the box. Recognising the increasingly severe threat that Britain faces, they must do the only thing open to them by adopting a bold strategy, one that proposes to create an increased level of amalgam of all three services into a more united defence force. One that employs the best qualities of the US Marine Corps, but that at the same time recognises the different demands of combat in different mediums and the value of unifying materiel and process, but acknowledge the existing service dependencies, such as Special

Operations Command and maritime logistics. This unification would require all senior staff officers of all the services to have a common understanding of all other services' theatres of war and combat techniques. And they must be able to do this within the context of the overall strategic priorities of Britain's defence at any given point in time.

If the Armed forces seriously proposed increased amalgamation, the politicians would know just how concerned the COS are and that their demands for higher levels of spending were not just posturing. As part of a *quid pro quo* they could demand a streamlining of the MoD, which would better support the new UK Defence Force. This would align them with Dominic Cummings, who has correctly identified that the MoD's procurement process requires a fundamental shift in mindset to become cost-effective. At the same time, the design to production time must be shortened significantly to move within the weapons' innovation cycles that are now visible in China and Russia's weapon development programmes.

2.5 THE UNIFICATION OF THE THREE SERVICES INTO A UK DEFENCE FORCE

A unified defence force is now a strategic imperative as next-generation complex weapons systems are now becoming more common in all theatres of war. As such, the sharing commonality of combat systems such as the CAMM (common anti-air modular missile) family programme would have enormous cost and deployment benefits. As the arms' race heats up and new weapons are coming online regularly, this would be a huge opportunity to develop new and effective capabilities that can then be sold on to our new trading partners and allies around the world.

Sadly, much as the logic is clear, the reality is that inter-service rivalry will undermine any such combined response by the COS. They will make some noises and once more become complicit in the failure to effectively defend Britain. However, that does not detract from what Global Forecaster should be doing in leading the thought process in the right direction. This 2020 Global Forecaster Security review is written in the hope that new right-brained (creative, bold and innovative) thought processes will rise to the fore in government and see the logic of the following arguments.

2.6 A STRONG UK DEFENCE FORCE EQUATES TO ENHANCED TRADE DYNAMICS

In a world of increasing threats from China and Russia, the growth of the UK defence forces and capabilities will give Britain both increased national security and the potential to build a stronger economy through strengthened trade relationships with other democratic nations across the globe.

However, one area of concern is selling lower-capability equipment to other nations that do not directly support the UK security agenda. Whilst export sales might make money, they potentially weaken the UK's defence performance, for example, the Type 31 frigate, which is not capable enough to be in the Royal Navy, is an export product whose sales potential is enhanced by its service in the fleet. Are these two mutually exclusive criteria? On the positive side, sales of the Type 31 would strengthen the supply chain by increasing shipbuilding capacity in the UK. Thus, whilst some UK programmes are much needed, they are pushed back in the queue by BAE to service their overseas sales, and the political kudos of doing so.

3.0 TOP-DOWN POST-BREXIT UK FOREIGN POLICY

3.1 POST-BREXIT BRITAIN IS THE ONLY WESTERN NATION IN AN EXPANSIVE PHASE

Notably, based on the *Five Stages of Empire*, Britain is the only nation of the old Western Christian Empire that is expanding post-regionalisation. As such, the stance the UK takes towards its foreign and defence policy will influence its allies significantly and impact the future of the world as we know it. Britain post-Brexit will require a new outward-looking national focus in its return to a global maritime paradigm, which will end an anomalous experiment with Continentalism, in other words, the economic dependence on the EU and the path to political sublimation. In doing so, Britain will return to its well-established, centuries-old model of a global maritime tradition with a policy of seeking stability and peace on the continent through military intervention where needed. Today, that is very specifically supporting NATO's defence against a very large Russian tank army.

In a world where China and Russia are on a path to conflict and coercion, the advantages and benefits of a strong UK Defence capability, able to project global power to develop and grow new trade relationships, are clear. Defence spending should not be viewed as wasteful but as something that will encourage significant economic returns and expansion.

There are six key elements that will redefine Britain's new role in the world:
1. The evolution of a modernised national identity defined as:
1. An independent sovereign state
2. An island nation
3. A democratic nation
4. A multiracial nation
5. A fully-functioning meritocracy
6. Our alliances, both bilateral and multilateral, such as the UK/US (intelligence, nuclear, aligned politics), NATO, FPDA, and Commonwealth and Dependent Territories.

2. An economy founded on free trade.
Brexit is in essence a return to the long-established model of a global maritime trading nation dependent on freedom of the seas to enact its trading policies.

3. Secure resource chains with access to commodities. This includes making sure the following key choke points are secured and protected:
1. Suez Canal
2. Cape of Good Hope
3. Cape Horn
4. Malacca Straights
5. Access to the China Seas
6. Future access to the Arctic trades routes (and to Japan).

4. **Our natural alliance with other democracies of the Anglosphere, Commonwealth and Europe**. The weaving and strengthening of alliances that contain China and constrict its ambitions should be of the utmost importance to Britain's foreign policy. These new alliances will also proffer the opportunity to build new trade relationships, especially in the Asian region, which has been the prime area of global growth.

5. **The enactment of a commodity resources strategy that secures resources needed by the UK from trusted allies while at the same time constricts the flow of resources to China to inhibit its economic growth and future military challenge to the West**. This strategy must be commenced now at the trough of the commodity cycle. Once prices begin to rise, consumer nations like the UK will have a tougher time negotiating trade agreements.

3.2 THE STATE OF THE WORLD TODAY AND IN THE NEXT DECADE

The world order with America as the single hegemonic power has now given way to a multi-polar world with three key features:

1. The decline of the West
2. The rise of China
3. An opportunistic Russia that seeks to exploit both maritime and continental weaknesses in Western control and influence zones.

3.2.1 THE DECLINE OF THE WEST

Human affairs are all about balance, both on a personal level and geopolitically between nations. Changes to the equilibrium always have consequences for a relationship. Some are benign, but some are far-reaching with, at times, dramatic and destructive results. In this ever-changing dynamic process, the key to maintaining harmony is to recognise and evaluate the nature of such shifts and to strive constantly to find ways to redress and maintain that crucial balance. To fail to recognise such threats risks the extinction of whole cultures.

The premise described in *Breaking the Code of History*, that the West (led by America) has been and still is in terminal decline, has over the past decade become an alarming reality. In such a circumstance, it is vital that sound strategic reasoning is applied to evaluate and understand the current and future geopolitical threats faced by Britain and the Western world. Additionally, it is critical that we ensure our limited resources are deployed wisely and proportionally, and that we accurately prioritise how we counter the various threats that we face.

This strategic imperative is further evidenced by the five-phase roadmap. Britain should be defined as in an expansive phase, which makes it the only nation in the Western world with such dynamic energy. As such it will inevitably find itself going head to head politically and economically with China in the near and long term. Additionally Britain will have an increasing leadership role within the Western nations, so where it goes others will follow.

3.2.2 THE RISE OF CHINA DEMANDS A POLICY OF ISOLATION AND CONTAINMENT

The time for engagement and rapprochement has passed. America is the last of the Western Christian Empires, but Britain is in a phase of ascension again. However, it is not of a magnitude that will shift this balance of power between East and West. The Asian Super Empire, led by China, is clearly also in its ascendancy. Management of this great power shift is the responsibility of current politicians and those of the next decade. If America continues its current economic path, its collapse will be precipitous and will consequently create a power vacuum that China's current youthful incarnation will quickly and aggressively step into, with potentially destructive consequences for all humanity.

The Global Forecaster Predictions since 2003 have been proven to be correct; China's power has grown at an astounding rate. To compound the threat to the West, China is now well and truly in the ascension to Empire phase of its development, having completed its Copy and Assimilation phase. Consequently, it is now innovating and creating new ways of owning war-winning technology. Foremost among these have been in cyberspace. Western assessments of China's economic prognosis will probably be a projection of its own decline and not see the underlying resilience of its economy, nor China's five-year plan to fully militarise its economy.

Such is the potential of China that this process represents a fundamental challenge not only to the Western way of life, but to the whole free world. In essence, this is a clash of civilisations between democratic and authoritarian states. America's pivot east demonstrates that the world's declining superpower is finally taking China seriously and is actively constructing alliances designed to contain China's expansion.

The only solution to the Chinese challenge over the next decade is to employ a similar strategy as in the Cold War to reduce the risk of conflict by matching China's expansion with the creation of a global political and military alliance led by America. If the strength and integrity of such an alliance were to match and even exceed China's growing power, the risks of war can be expected to decrease after the 2025 peak in the commodity cycle. Western defence spending is now required to invest in primary combat power. There will also be a need for sharing weapons technology with less developed allies such as India. Henceforth, the West must be accurately tuned to the signs of transformation in military affairs in China that could significantly and relatively quickly change the balance of power away from the West.

We should be very clear in our understanding of the magnitude of the Chinese challenge we face. Indeed, China is like no other threat that the West has ever seen since its rise 500 years ago. First, China aspires to be the world's third great sea power after Britain and the US. Unlike Britain and then America, which became demographically constrained as effective land powers (Britain in Europe and the US in Asia during the Korean and the Vietnam Wars), China's demographics make it potentially the greatest land power in history. This combination of potential land and sea power is unique in human history. The lessons from our past of German and Japanese aggressive expansions suggest that it could take an alliance of the whole world, including Africa, the Middle East and Latin America, to contain Chinese military build-up. Additionally, China's expansion and determination to use such newfound power will over the next few years become obvious to everyone.

Viewed in this context, China is by far the greatest of all the threats currently faced by Britain and the West with the potential to change the Western way of life drastically. Consequently, China demands the full attention of not only America but all its allies, including a rather comatose Europe. Britain has the opportunity to lead this process by using the laws around genocide, with respect to the Uighurs and Tibetans, to enforce company and national disengagement from China.

The first vital step is for the UK government and its leadership to quickly wake up to the Chinese threat and accept that the time for negotiation has passed. The time for a policy of containment is here. This includes the twin policies of a national commodity acquisition and containment of China via a constriction of its access to resources.

3.2.3 RUSSIA: A POLICY OF CONTAINMENT AND POTENTIAL RAPPROCHEMENT

By employing analyses from *Breaking the Code of History* and the five-phase roadmap in the form of *The Five Stages of Empire*, America and Europe should be considered as old systems. China is at the very opposite end of the spectrum, with a young expansive system that has great energy and, most importantly, the quality of innovation that generates revolutions in military affairs (RMAs) which in turn alter military balances.

Russia, in contrast, is also old within the empire cycle and thus as a potential enemy should be perceived as iterative rather than innovative. Most importantly, it is Putin who provides the national energy rather than the collective energy from its older declining population. Russia does not represent the determined and sustained threat it did in 1950. Also, its human and industrial resource bases, without the agglomerated nations of the USSR, are certainly not equivalent to the old empire.

This suggests a strategy of carrot and stick. The stick is the containment of Putin's aggressive proclivities through a strong military pushback and containment strategy that demonstrates Britain and the West are far from weak and that there are no cracks for opportunistic exploitation. The carrot would be the opening of the door to rapprochement and enticement away from Russia's alliance with China through economic cooperation. The goal should be to emulate the Anglo-French 1906 Entente Cordial that restructured the alliance as per 1914 to contain the rise of the Second Reich. The concept of bringing Russia back into the pre-1914 Western fold and thus surrounding China is a very powerful one in deterring a future WWIII scenario. Such an action would deprive China of Russia's resources, weakening her industrial economic base. It would also secure Europe from the Russian threat of conflict and allow Britain to focus on the expeditionary containment of China with maritime forces.

3.3 AMERICA: A REBALANCED SPECIAL RELATIONSHIP

The relationship between Britain and America since American independence has seen two distinct phases. The first was based on the hegemonic power of Britain and the rise of America's power that finally reached a degree of parity in 1917 when America loaned Britain the money it needed to continue fighting WWI. The second was from 1943 onwards when America became the dominant power in the partnership that became known as the 'Special Relationship'. We are now in the third phase, defined by the terminal decline of America and the rise of Britain. Whilst America is both militarily and economically more powerful than Britain, one of the defining qualities of this new phase of the relationship is that Britain's expansionist energy is very different to America's contracting energy.

The manifestation of this new phase should be an ever-closer relationship between the two nations. One in which Britain's relative strength and influence will inevitably increase. Critical to Britain's future value in the American relationship will be a significantly increased military capability. Additionally, as the moral framework of the American version of democracy fractures in decline it will be up to Britain to create a new modernised version of a free multicultural meritocracy from which to positively influence the free world.

3.4 THE EU: A RETURN TO BRITAIN'S OLD EUROPEAN FOREIGN POLICY

Britain's focus should be to ensure the economic stability of the EU and, most importantly, its security through NATO against Russian threats. However, it should be recognised that for an initial period post-Brexit the EU will not support or encourage Britain's economic success for fear that other nations will follow in Britain's footsteps. Whilst the Russian threat persists, a strengthened UK defence capability and its ability to support NATO's defence of Europe will provide strong leverage for the resolution of any economic frictions between the EU and Britain.

3.5 THE NATIONS OF THE PACIFIC BASIN: THE POTENTIAL FOR NEW ALLIANCES AND NEW TRADE PARTNERSHIPS

The Asia Pacific region is the centre for the world's economic expansion and is the base for the rise of China. This allows the potential for Britain to play a major role in the Pacific alliance that seeks to contain China and in so doing strengthens economic ties with India, Japan and Australia in the form of new trade deals. Once again, a powerful military will provide leverage in this process and the opportunity to sell UK weapons that will strengthen the UK's industrial military complex.

3.6 THE MIDDLE EAST: AN OPPORTUNITY FOR NEW, STRENGTHENED ECONOMIC RELATIONSHIPS

With the new Arab-Israeli alliance, the centre of the region has entered a new phase of stability that provides an opportunity for Britain to strengthen ties in the region. This is especially true in regard to Israel with whom diplomatic relationships have been strained as Britain has to date favoured its Arab relationships. This has the added advantage that this group is set against Iran, the one regional foe that Britain faces. Once more, military alignment will have economic advantages.

3.7 AFRICA: A RETURN TO THE FORGOTTEN CONTINENT

Africa has once more become the forgotten continent in Western foreign policy. However, to China it is a vital resource basin, upon which it has planned its hegemonic expansion. With the withdrawal of Western interests in Africa, the vacuum created allowed China to expand its political and military tentacles across the continent. That dynamic strategy should now be inverted by Britain whose Commonwealth links and commonality to their democracies provides the opportunity for strengthened economic ties and the benefit of providing alternative financing options to those offered by China. The trade route around southern Africa will continue to be critical and, as such, relationships with South Africa, and support for its democratic origins, should be of the highest importance.

A prime example of where Britain should commence this strategic support and intervention is in Mozambique and Tanzania, where ISIS has gained a significant foothold and is once more terrorising local populations whilst overwhelming government resources. Both governments have requested support and UK Special Forces intervention could be extremely effective. Notably, both nations occupy a significant portion of the Eastern Africa seaboard, critical real-estate when it comes to the containment of Chinese aspirations in Africa.

3.8 LATIN AMERICA: A RETURN TO AN OLD FRIENDSHIP

Britain once had a prime relationship with many of the Latin American nations. This ended in 1917 when loans from America were predicated on Britain handing its prime hegemonic relationship to America. With that transition went the main economic dynamics. Today, as American influence contracts, there will be new opportunities for Britain to grow its trading relations with the continent.

3.9 TIMING OF THE NEXT MAJOR WAR

The concepts in *Breaking the Code of History* explained that the majority of wars are always driven by the need for resources (see the 54-year Kondratiev Cycle). The current cycle commenced in 2000, rallied until 2010, and has since been in a deep correction. This should end in the next 12 months, before an extremely powerful inflationary rally into a spiked peak around 2025-2027.

There are two main risks associated with the Commodity cycle. First, it is the current dip in commodity prices that allows for the opportunity of a potential rapprochement with Putin as Russia's finances deteriorate. The alternative is that Putin seeks a regional conflict to distract attention away from his domestic political failures. Second, the impending 2025–27 peak is the point where commodity friction with China is most likely to catalyse a global conflict.

Below: This diagram of current and previous K wave cycles provided by Tony Plumber, shows that we are currently in a price correction that will bottom out in the next six months. This will then be followed by a very aggressive price rally into a peak in 2025–27.

This peak will be associated with the greatest risk of global war since 1914. However if we can deter conflict through full spectrum deterrence during the peak, then we will have 25 plus years of commodity deflation to resolve and integrate China into a new world.

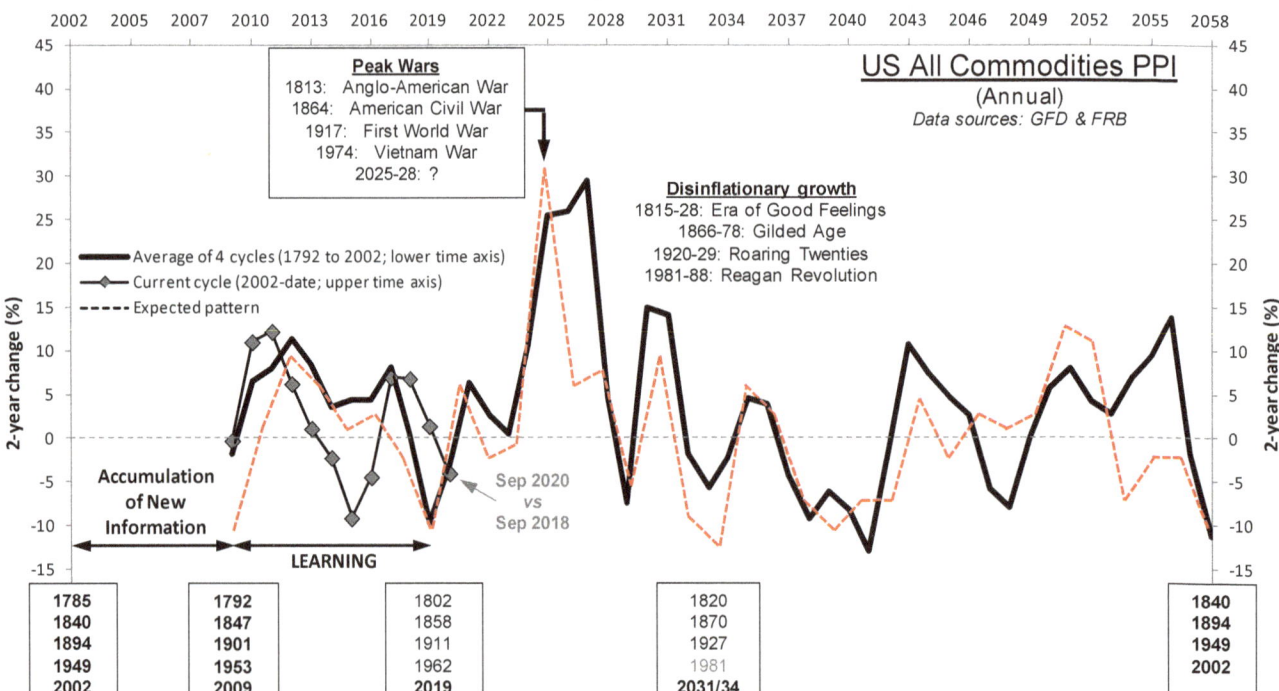

3.10 SUMMARY OF KEY THREATS TO THE UK OVER THE NEXT DECADE

1. **China: an expanding nation that represents the biggest threat to the free world**

2. **Russia: a regional foe that could be politically mitigated and brought back into the Western fold**

3. **Iran: to a minor degree as it seeks to close the straits of Hormuz. However, the expansion required to deter Russia and China will minimise the Iranian threat.**

With the timing of the next Commodity cycle, and the evidence that China's five-year plan is very similar to that of Hitler's four-year plan, Britain has to have radically restructured and redeployed its defence forces by 2025. If Britain fails to do this, it will be too late to deter the inevitable aggression that could lead to WWIII.

3.11 THE IMPACT OF CLIMATE CHANGE

Global Forecaster predicted in 2003 that climate change was a man-made phenomena and highlighted a route map that we would experience as its impacts became more severe. It further highlighted that the rates of change were vastly underestimated and that they would keep increasing. As we are at the point where the rate of change of global warming is accelerating far faster than current linear models predict, this is being driven by the oceanic heat sinks which have to date absorbed the increased atmospheric energy, but which are now starting to increase in temperature. In so doing, they are feeding change back into our climate and the melting of the land ice is accelerating, with associated sea level changes. As the impacts become more severe we will experience a quantum jump leap in climate change and today we are just beginning to experience these effects.

Geostrategically this means that we will see disruptions to food supplies and sea-level changes that will increase political tensions and the risks of proxy conflict in some very unlikely locations. Additionally it means that the Arctic will open up and become both contested and provide new trade routes to Asia that will need to be protected by the Royal Navy and that will simultaneously provide egress points into Russia. In summary, climate change will only exacerbate the current geopolitical tensions, increasing the risk of a global conflict in 2025-27.

4.0 UK DEFENCE FORCE STRUCTURING

4.1 THE REQUIREMENT FOR THE UK'S KEY STRATEGIC DEFENCE CAPABILITIES COMMENSURATE WITH THE FOREIGN POLICY STRATEGY

Whilst this review's recommended increase in military capabilities may seem very high in percentage terms, one should remember that over the past two decades the UK's defence capability has been run down to the bone in every service. Simultaneously, the threat environment has jumped by many multiples. There are four key areas relating to the defence commands. The following suggestions in their respective categories are areas I believe should receive specific attention. More specific details are given in the Appendices.

4.1.1 STRATEGIC NUCLEAR DETERRENCE

1. **The continuation of the effective last-ditch strategic nuclear deterrent by the Royal Navy**.

2. **The development of new low-yield nuclear weapons** (100-200 tonnes) mounted on stealthy cruise missiles that allow a proportional full-spectrum response to any attempts to use small nuclear weapons for strategic advantage.

4.1.2 MARITIME (ROYAL NAVY)

1. A multi-layered underwater early warning system, like SOSUS (Sound Surveillance System), all around the UK.

2. Control the surface and sub-surface of all adjacent waters extending across the North Atlantic and into the South Atlantic, specifically the UK-Iceland Gap, to bottle up the Russian navy. Place the emphasis on the increasing use of drones with persistence and strike capabilities, and the opportunity to operate these autonomously.

3. Project submarine power into the Russian nuclear fleet's bastions in the Northern Seas.

4. Secure global sea lanes and choke points.

5. Enforce trade protection, counter piracy, illegal immigration and arms' smuggling, illegal fishing and environmental policing.

6. Project power to contain Chinese expansion beyond the First Island Chain.

7. Conduct expeditionary amphibious war games in littoral zones to support the above objectives of the Royal Navy.

Opposite, top: A pair of F-35Bs from the RAF (top) and US Marine Corps (USMC) formation flying over England. Although the F-35B is less capable than the F-35C, it has a 25Mw lift fan that could in future power a laser that would greatly enhance fleet and national defence from incoming ballistic missile threats.
Credit: UK MoD © Crown copyright 2019

Below: Pictured in formation are, RFA *Tideforce* (lead), HMS *Northumberland* (left), USS *Truxtun* (far left), HMS *Dragon* (right), USS *Philippine Sea* (far right) with HMS *Queen Elizabeth* at the rear during Exercise *Westlant 19*.

HMS *Queen Elizabeth* is the biggest ship ever constructed for the Royal Navy. Exercise *Westlant 19* puts this formidable warship and her embarked F-35 fighter jets through their paces on the US Eastern Seaboard.

As well as testing the capability of HMS *Queen Elizabeth* and the F-35, *Westlant 19* is an excellent opportunity to strengthen ties with one of our most important allies: the United States.
Credit: UK MoD © Crown copyright 2019

Opposite, top: Royal Air Force C130J Hercules conducting low-light refuelling with an Airbus Voyager Air tanker over England. In air refuelling it is critical to extend the range of our combat fighters. However, the RAF needs to develop a fleet of stealthy drone tankers that can operate in the forward and contested airspace, to further increase combat range.
Credit: UK MoD © Crown copyright 2018

Below: RAF Fylingdales is a small unit on the North Yorkshire Moors and was first declared operational in 1963 as one of three radar sites in the Ballistic Missile Early Warning System (BMEWS), the other two sites being in Alaska and Greenland.

The site was originally dominated by three 'Golf Balls' which housed mechanical tracking radars. In the early 1990s, the old radars were replaced by a much more capable Solid State Phased Array Radar (SSPAR), which underwent another upgrade that was completed in 2007. The SSPAR can keep track of many hundreds of space objects per minute out to a range of 3,000 nautical miles. The radar software is designed to ignore targets that do not behave like a rocket being launched or a satellite in orbit.
Credit: UK MoD © Crown copyright 2018

4.1.3 RAF AND SPACE FORCE

1. Control of space above the UK, Royal Navy and expeditionary operations zones (air and missile defence of homeland and combat zones). Space is the next high ground of modern warfare, with the emphasis on the increasing use of drones with persistence and strike capabilities, and the opportunity to operate these autonomously.

2. Maintenance of satellite sensors, GPS and weapons systems.

3. Maritime patrols in support of the Royal Navy.

4. Long-range strike capability of the RAF to deliver precise conventional and nuclear ordinance.

5. Tactical air support over combat zones.

4.1.4 ARMY

1. Should support European allies against Russia.

2. Greater focus on amphibious warfare to support the Royal Navy. This raises the question of enlarging the Royal Marines' strength.

3. A return to global deployments in Africa and the Pacific basin in support of our regional allies (for example, Japan, South Korea, Australia, India and South Africa).

4. Civil order and disaster relief.

4.2 THE DANGERS AND OPPORTUNITIES OF REVOLUTIONS IN MILITARY AFFAIRS

The process of challenge to an established hegemonic power has historically always instigated a new arms' race that seeks to overturn the old order of battle. Today, that arms' race is in full swing. Consequently, RMAs are unfolding at a staggering rate and threaten to upset the global power balance. A new rising empire is always quicker than the older systems it seeks to challenge due to its wish to harness innovation as a military advantage. These new RMAs seriously risk making current weapon systems and forces obsolete. The main focus of current and future RMAs are as follows:

1. **Redeployment of current weapons into new applications**. The Chinese have developed a class of weapons to destroy US carriers using short and intermediate ballistic missiles. These will prevent the US from accessing the South China Seas. Initially, the warheads were manoeuvrable re-entry vehicles, but new hypersonic warheads are being deployed that will considerably increase the system's lethality. The potential of this weapons platform for global maritime control is obvious if long-range ballistic missiles like the DF-421 are equipped with similar warheads. This would mean that the PLN (People's Liberation Navy) could hit ships 12,000 to 15,000 kilometres (km) away. To give you an idea of this distance, 15,000 km is roughly equivalent to the width of three US-sized countries laid side by side. Once ships required anti-aircraft guns to protect themselves. Today, every warship will need ABMs to protect itself. Based on this, the Royal Navy should upgrade the weapon systems on all of its vessels.

2. **Cyber capabilities** that were originally created by the Chinese to steal Western intellectual property (IP). Out of its huge population, a specialist force of 200,000

high-IQ individuals were first unleashed to steal Western IP. This evolved into a full spectrum capability, emulated by all major combatants, that can penetrate critical infrastructures and networked weapon systems. Meanwhile, information networks are continuing to be more complex and effective, giving all those involved in the battle space more real-time information, which should make them more deadly. However, this technology is also an Achilles heel if an enemy uses offensive cyber capabilities against such networks, because it could bring about the potential calamitous collapse of the other side in a war. Hence, this area requires constant focus and attention to ensure a capable offensive and defensive capability. Cyber capabilities are no substitute for kinetic systems, but rather part of an integrated full-spectrum response.

3. **Stealth**. Increased lethality on the battlefield has forced a new camouflage revolution that we call stealth, in thermal, visual and across the full electromagnetic spectrum (ES). Currently, continuing the old WWI adage of 'if you cannot be seen you are less likely to be attacked', the US leads this area of new technology, although Britain's Astute-class submarine is possibly the stealthiest of its kind. Notably, this technology has been spreading across many nations and military applications and is a trend that can only be expected to continue. However, the impending development of quantum radars has the potential to negate this technology upon which a significant Western advantage is based.

4. **Underwater, land and air unmanned drones**. The deployment of combat robots in all aspects of warfare is an imminent combat revolution. One very good example is the Russian Status-6 submarine drones, with nuclear engines and warheads, that will require new sub-surface defence sensors and weapons to counter effectively.

5. **Artificial intelligence** is close at hand, and it will be a relatively small step to give unmanned vehicles full autonomy in the future.

6. **Quantum technology** threatens to revolutionise secure communications, code-breaking and sensors that can detect submarines.

7. **Hypersonics** are delivery systems that can fly to their target at speeds greater than five times the speed of sound to evade interception, making them almost impossible to intercept with the majority of current anti-missiles in service.

8. **Laser technology**, led by the US Navy, is now close to deployment and will change the battle space it dominates. Whilst susceptible to bad weather, they could be a very effective counter to saturation attacks and hypersonic missiles. However, it will require greater power supplies and, as such, warships and land vehicles will need to encompass increasingly larger power plants at the heart of their designs.

9. **Rail-gun technology**, also led by the US Navy, has potentially great promise but is being held up by finding the right material for the rails that can survive the very high temperatures involved.

10. **The weaponisation of space**. The high ground is always where the advantage lies, and in Earth's case, the ultimate high ground is space. Space is one battle space that the UK has not focused on and one that we urgently need to address.

Taken as a whole, the range and speed of the new *RMAs* will make the majority of the UK's current forces obsolete, which demands major new investment in the nation's national defence forces. On the bright side, the development and deployment of new weapons, such as lasers, could shift the power balance back in favour of Western forces and deter Chinese aggression.

4.3 ASSESSMENT OF THE UK'S CURRENT FORCE STRUCTURE.

4.3.1. BRITAIN'S INTELLIGENCE SERVICES

Britain's intelligence services have quite correctly continued to receive relatively generous funding over the past decade from an absolute spending perspective. However, it would appear that our capacity does not match the expanding multiple threats, especially in the cyber domain, but also in the traditional intelligence services where we encounter three major threats that require ongoing monitoring: Islamic fundamentalism, Russia and China. Whilst Russia and Islamic fundamentalism are understood threats, the new threat provided by China, along with its global footprint, will require a massive enlargement of our intelligence capabilities. To respond appropriately, the government needs to at least double its organisational strength in the intelligence services and in the case of GCHQ (Government Communications Headquarters) possibly by more than that. Strategic and tactical intelligence have been and always will be at the heart of a war-winning capability.

4.3.2 ROYAL NAVY

The Royal Navy emerges as relatively the best of the three services in its design of suitable weapons platforms for future threats, in the face of horrendous cost-cutting. To its credit, it has managed to design, build and operate at least two world-class weapons platforms and seeks to once more re-establish air power at sea, with all its associated power projection capability. However, the Royal Navy is in crisis and in urgent need of investment and expansion. It is desperate for more platforms, as, regardless of how capable each one now is, they cannot be in two places at once. Hence, our recommendation is an immediate expansion to a 100-ship Royal Navy. Coincident with this ship expansion, the Navy has to urgently solve a major shortage of manpower.

4.3.3 ROYAL AIR FORCE

The Royal Air Force currently has the capability to defend our airspace against Russian incursions and deploy tactical strike capabilities to a low-intensity war. However, it has been guilty of failing to demonstrate the foresight to create an integrated air defence of the UK, using combinations of missiles and fighter aircraft. Additionally, if it is to support a new mobile British Army, it will need to significantly enhance its heavy lift capability. There is also a strong case to give the RAF the equivalent of a 10-plane strong strategic bomber force of B-21s for maritime control and strategic nuclear delivery as a backup to Trident. Meanwhile, space is the next high ground of the modern battleground, and it would seem that there is a risk that Britain itself feels precluded by a lack of investment. However, this is an area where new investment and cooperation with the US, including technology transfers, could bear significant fruit. An example would be the creation of a new Missile Defence Command, integrated into the RAF's responsibility for air defence of the UK.

4.3.4 THE ARMY

The Army's condition, after almost a decade and half of continuous land operations, is lamentable, and consequently, it is the worst positioned of the three services. It is now focused on a light intervention role and has abandoned the concept that it could be involved in a high-intensity war. This is a critical misjudgement that needs to be corrected urgently. Additionally, with the trend in battlefield innovations, there is an opportunity for the British Army to create a new force concept that can deploy a Heavy Combat Division and ideally, corps-sized force to the point where they are needed rapidly. One can only conclude that, to execute its role in defence of the nation, the Army is in urgent need of overhaul and expansion.

To rectify the Army's condition, one has to ask why it has fallen into such disrepair. One cause is the ever-increasing politicisation of senior officers after the Afghanistan War. This trend has filtered out the maverick straight-talking generals needed to look forward with capable and independent thought. Without this type of leader, innovation at a senior level will continue to be absent. The second is the legacy caused by a state of trauma post-Afghanistan five years ago, not dissimilar to that which the US Army faced after the Vietnam War.

The Army seems to lack a new younger leadership that could create a more effective force, similar to the one prepared to confront Hitler's Germany (influenced by Fuller and Liddell Hart) as seen at the end phases of the Cold War. One can only conclude that the very nature of leadership and the quality of the Army generals needs to be enhanced to ensure that it can develop a realistic force structure capable of fighting a high-intensity war. It should be noted that the pattern of the Army being unready to fight the next war has been a regular theme in the past century.

This problem, which might impact current events, is undoubtedly rooted in the very tribalistic nature of the Army's regimental structure. To be clear, during a period of ruthless and unfounded cuts, regiments have become defensive in order to save themselves. I strongly believe in the power of the regimental system to create effective land-fighting forces by calling on the traditions of the past to motivate combat capability, but under such circumstances the tribal fractures are working against the overall capability of the Army. The Army, to its credit, has recognised the problem and thus members of the General Staff who are full colonels or above do not wear regimental cap badges to identify their regimental origins. However, they are allowed to wear their colour berries that denote regimental backgrounds, defeating the objective! As such, more work is needed to reduce regimental tribalism and increase overall full-spectrum combat capability of the British Army.

Additionally, the complexity of the Army's weapons is far below that of the other services, perhaps because the Army allows its senior officers to rise to power without an appreciation of modern technology (with the exception of artillery and engineering officers), and the rate at which it is evolving. The question that springs to mind then is: Is this a repeat of the post-WWI old horse versus tank paradigm, in a modern form?

This is compounded by the peacetime paradigm of generals rising to the top with an absence of management skills apart from relevant large-scale command skills.

Above: Drones, both cheap, small and numerous, and large, complex and expensive, will soon come to dominate the battle space in all mediums. The application of small swarm deployed anti-personnel drones in built-up areas is but one development that will rebalance technology over a numerous and determined enemy.
Credit: UK MoD © Crown copyright 2020

Opposite, top: The formidable British Challenger 2 main battle tank of the 1st Royal Tank Regiment, at speed in the Omani landscape. The mooted scrapping of the Army's Heavy Combat Divisions would remove a key element of Britain's full-spectrum response. It is critical that these divisions be kept in service, and that simultaneously Britain develops new weapons and tactics associated with new and more powerful heavy combat forces.
Credit: UK MoD © Crown copyright 2020

Below: The Royal Marines have a long history in specialising in light force projection. However, the time has come to increase the missile density and capabilities of light forces in both the Marines and the Army to give them far greater combat power and striking range, both surface to surface and surface to air.
Credit: UK MoD © Crown copyright 2020

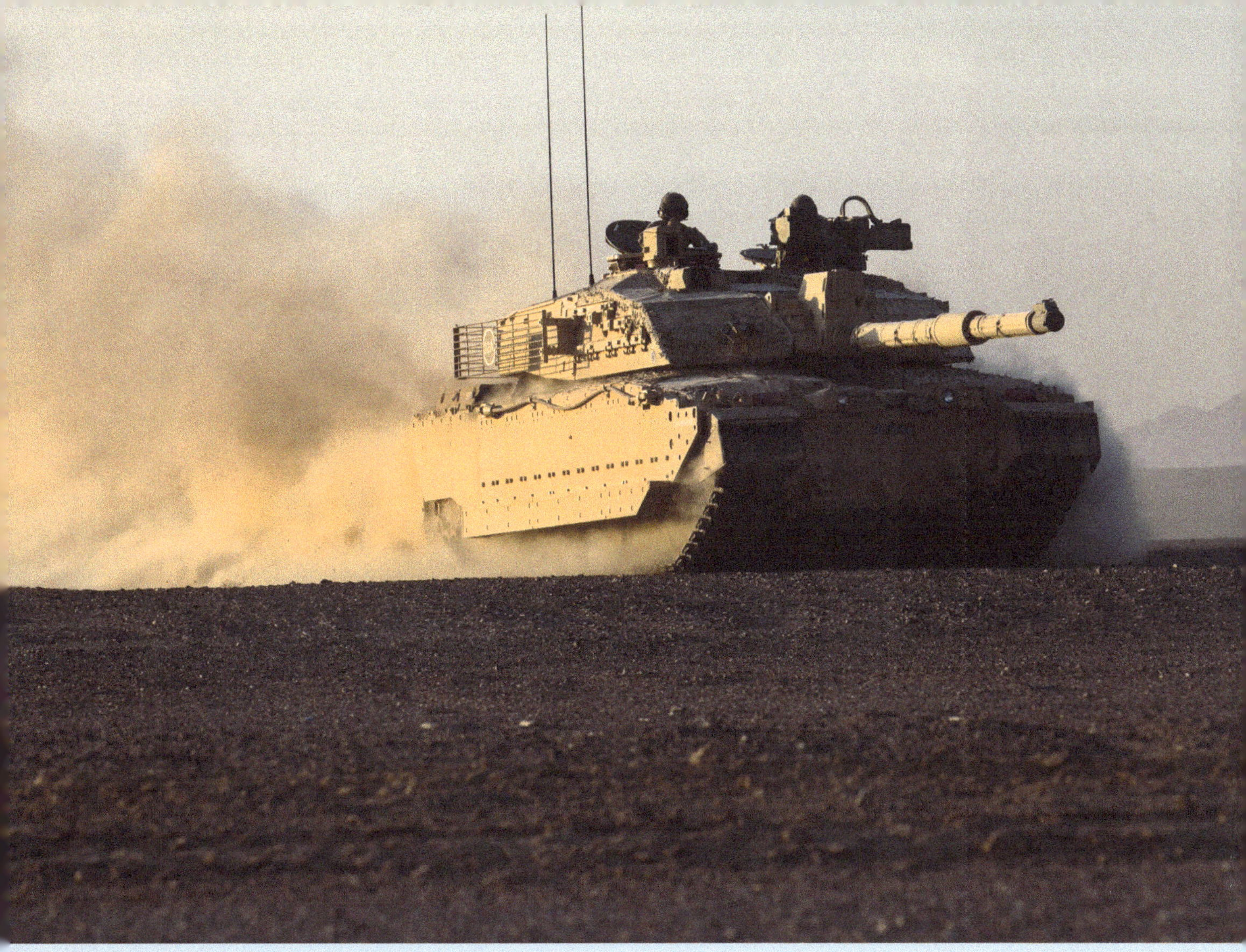

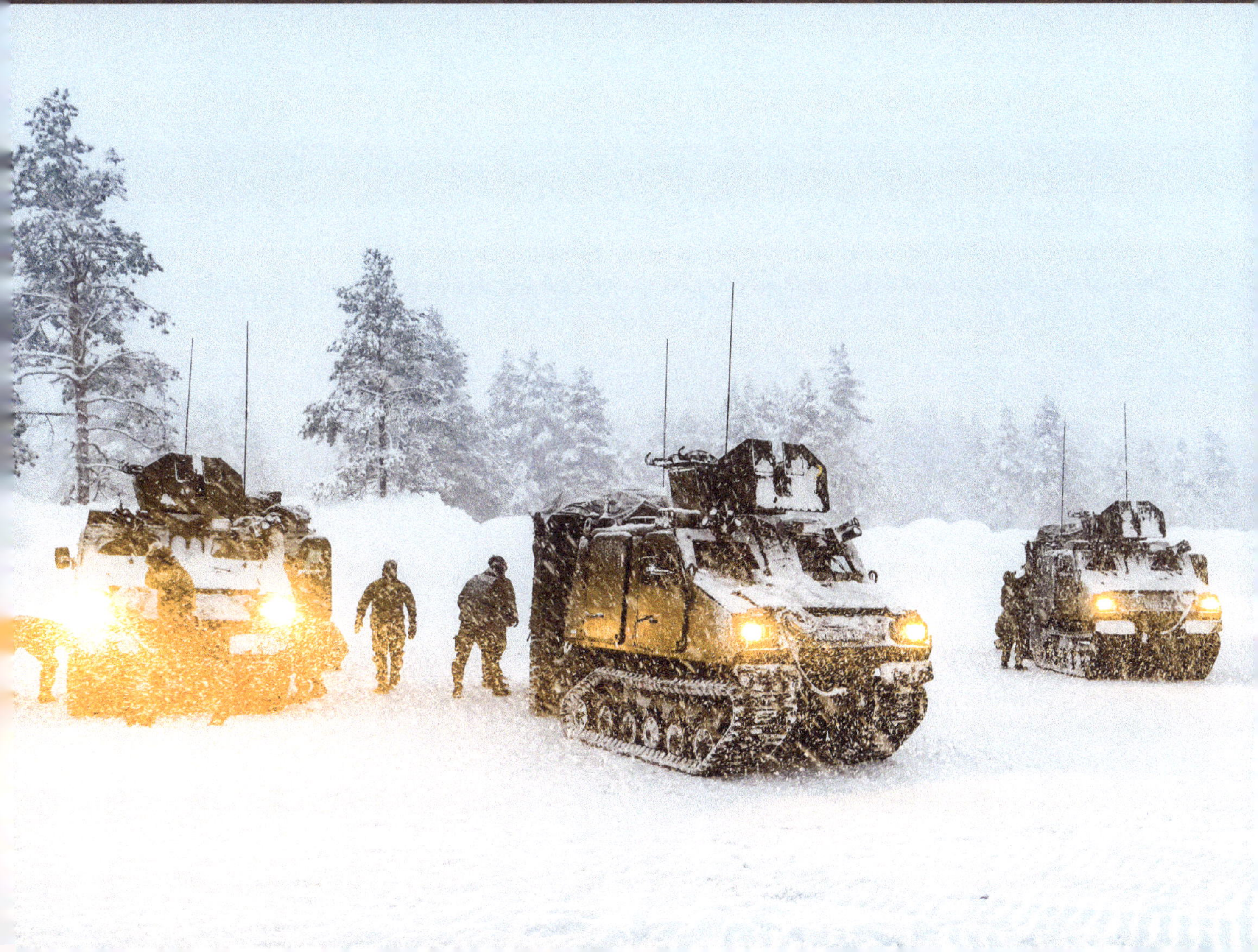

4.4 A NEW UK DEFENCE FORCE

The suggested force structure below is designed to give increased depth to the ability of UK forces to respond to the right threat with the right tools and maximise the deployment of our forces to the great effect. Recent examples are the use of a high-end air defence destroyer like the Type-45 on anti-piracy missions, or the use of Euro fighters as tactical bombers in Libya after scrapping the much better-adapted Harrier GR7 for the task, or escorting transiting Russian warships with survey and support ships. This sends a clear message of weakness to our enemies. There is also a significant negative cost implication of this misuse of assets

4.4.1 STRATEGIC NUCLEAR DETERRENCE

The continuation of an effective last-ditch nuclear deterrent is critical to Britain's security. To achieve this there are three key components that need to be implemented.

1. **The continuation and effectiveness of the strategic national deterrent** by the Royal Navy. This means ensuring the integrity of the active ballistic missile submarine with delousing procedures and escort vessels, in addition to ensuring that it remains undetectable once at sea.

2. **New SOSUS networks.** The threat of the new Status-6 submarine drone demands new and extensive SOSUS networks (the Cold War codename given to the passive sonar system developed by the US Navy to track Soviet submarines around the UK in multiple layers). Such a system would also support the SSBNs.

3. **The deployment of new low-yield nuclear weapons** (100-200 tonnes) mounted on stealthy cruise missiles that allow a proportional full-spectrum response to any Russian attempts to use a small nuclear weapon for strategic advantage, deployed by the Royal Navy Army and the RAF. To those not familiar with the basis of Cold War deterrence, this flexible response is as vital today as it was as deterrent in the Cold War, because unless Britain is able to respond to an aggressive escalation in kind it is either forced to escalate itself, with the risk of total war, or retreat or surrender.

4.4.2 MARITIME (ROYAL NAVY)

The structure of the Royal Navy is in place to accept new weapons systems and to act as a base for expansion. However, as the frontline in Britain's maritime defence it needs considerable and urgent investment to return it to a combat-capable force that can cope with a peer threat like the Russian or Chinese navy.

1. **Increased manpower** starting immediately to enact an increase of 50%.

2. **Take the current fleet to full strength.** Ensure the current fleet is fully operative and effectively manned and provisioned with sufficient supplies of ammunition and spares.

3. **Stealth technology** should be applied to all ships of the fleet in all domains, visually, sonically, thermally and in the EM spectrum.

4. **Equipped with 48 F35-Bs**, for example, two full carrier Air Wings of F35-C fully deployed with air-to-surface missile capabilities, in-air refuelling capabilities and V22 resupply and marine insertion tilt rotors.

5. **Build more ships to deploy a 100-ship fleet**

- **12 new batch 2 Type-45** ballistic missile defence ships, equipped with an ABM version of the Sea Viper or SM-6 missiles
- **30 new Type-26s** and upgrade the 31 frigates on order from export to more heavily armed ships
- **6 new Astute-class submarines**, to make a total of 12
- **Drone ships**: build a new class of medium-sized stealthy drone battery ships to operate on the outer layers of the fleet's defence, acting as force multipliers
- **12 small coastal air-independent subs** and or 1,000-tonne hunter-killer drones.
- **16-20 new coastal corvettes** which are fast and heavily armed and highly automated in the 1,500 to 2,000-tonne displacement range , to patrol out to the 200-mile limit and maintain the border integrity of Britain's maritime zones (aka Norwegian designs).
- **More logistic support ships**, in new stealthy designs that do not give away the fleet's position.

6. **Enhanced weaponry**
   - **Greater weapon density** on each ship, for example, Mk41 launches on all ships, more missile silos, more CIWS (close-in weapon system) per ship
   - **Enact a policy of distributed lethality** through all fleet and auxiliary ships
   - **New long-range surface-to-surface missiles** to outreach current Chinese and Russian missiles
   - **Give the carriers their own air-defence capability**, either Aster 15 or Sea Ceptor and upgrades to ABM defence as soon as possible
   - **Build a more powerful CIWS** and increase the number on each ship
   - **Deploy laser and rail gun technologies** asap, for example, lasers to equip ships and F35-Bs
   - **Deploy Sea Ceptor** in quad-packed Mk41 launchers of the Type 26s and 31s
   - **Modify the Sylvester launcher** to compatibility with Mk41 launchers
   - **Deploy anti-sub RUM-139 ASROC** rocket-propelled torpedo (stingray replacing the US Mk 46 torpedo).

7. **Royal Marines**
   The Royal Marines, as a lightly armed amphibious force, for a time were outmoded if faced by a well-armed defence. However, the US Marines are adapting part of their forces into a heavily armed missile capable force, that can land (ideally via covert insertion techniques) and then project maritime and air control to impede an enemy's movement. This development points the way to enhance the Royal Marines combat capability and should be implemented as soon as possible.

4.4.3 ROYAL AIR AND SPACE FORCE

1. **The Royal Air Force remains an aeroplane centric force**, with a structure that favours a pilot culture that was perpetuated by Jock Stirrup. Although it has recently embraced the role of space command, its failure to develop surface-to-air missile forces as an essential part of Britain's air defence capability demonstrates an institutional blindness that needs to be purged if its new role in space control is to be successful. Similarly to the Royal Navy, the RAF's structure allows relatively swift expansion, although its ethos will require a major adjustment to the new missile age.

2. **The full order of 148 F35s needs to be purchased**. This should be comprised as follows: at least 60% should be F35-Bs with their vertical lift-off maritime capabilities and 25MW lift fan that could power an airborne laser; and 40% should be F35-Cs (but not F35-As) as the F35-C is the most capable of the three platforms in terms of range and load-carrying capability.

3. **Develop a UK space launch capability** based in Scotland facilitating the launch of and operation of space lasers and advanced sensors.

4. **Deploy a long-range strategic conventional strike** capability to maritime and land targets via a new generation of hypersonic and stealthy cruise missiles, delivered from a long-range stealthy platform such as the B21 Raider.

5. **The deployment of a stealth drone** refuelling planes such as the Boeing Mq-25 Stingray to allow the F35 force deeper penetration capabilities.

6. **The development and deployment of a UK air and space defence system** capable of intercepting both incoming ballistic missiles and high- and low-altitude hypersonic missiles. This would be based on US missile technologies deployed on land and in space.

Opposite, top: An RAF Typhoon moves to intercept a Russian military aircraft heading towards British airspace off the coast of north-west Scotland. Several QRA RAF fighter jets were scrambled to intercept the unidentified Russian aircraft after they tried to enter British airspace.

The unidentified aircraft were later revealed to be Tupolev Tu-95 Bears – Russian aircraft used both as strategic bombers and long-range maritime patrol planes.

Flying in formation, two pairs (from RAF Coningsby and RAF Lossiemouth) approached the aircraft before withdrawing, while the third pair finished the job of forcing them to change course.
Credit: UK MoD © Crown copyright 2020

Below: Night shoot of Sentry AEW. Mk 1 aircraft at RAF Waddington. Officially designated Sentry AEW. Mk 1 in RAF service, but commonly known as E-3D, Sentry is an airborne early warning (AEW) and command-and-control aircraft. It monitors airspace to provide threat detection of adversary aircraft and situational awareness on friendly assets.
Credit: UK MoD © Crown copyright 2018

4.4.4 THE ARMY

The Army is the one service that needs a complete force restructuring both in terms of organisation and weapons and ethos. However, in some areas it is already making excellent progress. The best example of which is the deep battle concept of extending its strike range deep into an enemy's territory, such that it then constricts the enemy's capability to operate in the near battle space. The formation of 77 Brigade and its cyber capabilities is one part of a broad development that will employ cyber, artificial intelligence, stealth drones with long loiter capabilities and deep-fire capabilities that can reach many hundreds of miles into enemy territory.

However, there still remains the need for a fundamental reorganisation of capacity into a three-phase force development programme.

4.4.4.1 THE OPTIMISATION OF CURRENT FORCES

Recognising that a major transition in land military combat technology and tactics is upon us, the first step is to optimise the current light and heavy forces for three key roles.

1. **Defence of the UK against light or heavy attack**.

2. **The projection of heavy tanks divisions into Europe** to deter any potential aggression by Russia.

3. **Ensuring that the Airborne Mobile Division** is able to deploy swiftly anywhere in the world to effect/deter a proxy war, but is upgraded with a much higher density of missile systems, as proposed by the new US Marine Corps Littoral Combat Units.

4. **The Light Forces** should be similarly upgraded with higher levels of missile systems to increase hitting power and be globally deployable from UK bases and Royal Navy assets in addition to being based with our allies.

4.4.4.2 THE CREATION OF A NEW HIGH-TECH HEAVY MOBILE FORCE

In the 1920 to 1930s both Fuller and Liddell Hart developed the model of a blitzkrieg war: one that the British Army ignored and the German army implemented, to Europe's great cost. Today, we face an urgent need to create a new form of Army Division based around a new common tank/armoured personnel system, as outlined in the Future of the Tank (see Appendices). This would be an armoured division that would be technology heavy with drones and swarm systems and fully air transportable, both over a long range by helium airships point to point, or into combat by heavy lift tilt rotors. The essence of this new force is a very high-tech organisation that matches that of the Royal Navy and the RAF. As this concept becomes proven, it will become the basis for the new fighting forces and will become the core of the New Army Model.

4.4.4.3 THE CREATION OF A HOME FORCE

The Army arm of the armed forces would use military training and skills to develop a large force whose main role would be the leadership and skill development of the young, who would otherwise be unemployed, in a model that would be something akin to voluntary National Service. This Home force would develop national values of service, self-growth and leadership that would develop the youth of today into more effective members of society. It would also provide a basis for disaster relief and the support of society. The budget should predominantly come from the unemployment budget.

Critics of such a Home force might argue that there would still be many unemployed. Indeed in the depression ahead it is highly conceivable that we could have 3-5 million unemployed in the years ahead. So how big could such a Home force become? Given sufficient resources it could easily be of the order of 500,000 and even grow to 1 million in a few years. What would be critical is that it would employ the young, and educate them with skills confidence, leadership and national values that would then feed back into a more productive society for the future of the nation. Additionally, as Britain seeks to create a meritocratic and multiracial society, the experience of being part of an organisation with a strong core ethos of equality and integration would also feed back into national energy pride and self-belief that will only strengthen Britain's future.

Below: Russia's development of the state-of-the-art T14 main battle tank is a reminder to the West that Russia continues to seek to threaten Europe with its guards tank army. To fail to deter such an overt threat would be a grave mistake.
Credit: 2020 iStockphoto LP

5.0
THE RIGHT EXPENDITURE LEVELS VERSUS THE RISKS WE FACE

5.1 HISTORICAL PERSPECTIVES

Historically, democracies have not been good at anticipating rising aggressor nations and preparing a commensurately strong defence. Furthermore, there is a long-established trend (not unique to the UK) of preparing for the last war rather than anticipating the next. Consequently, the 2015 Strategic Defence Report built in limitations and flaws that were of an institutional nature and repeated the errors of the past century's military planning. To avoid what could prove to be a terrible error, we have to form a defence policy from basic principles commensurate with the external threats that we face.

The big question is what percentage of its GDP should Britain be spending on defence that is appropriate to the current threat? The answer starts with guidance from the past and plots of expenditure levels over the past 115 years. The first observation is that, surprisingly, up to now the correlation between the percentage of GDP expenditure and military manning levels is very high as the ratio of the manpower cost to higher technology up to now has been relatively constant. However, with increased automation in combat systems I would expect this established ratio to change going forward.

The second observation is that the massive spikes in GDP spending and manpower in WWI and WWII both consumed roughly 50% of GDP for their duration. Irrespective of the horrendous human cost these wars entailed, the spikes are a clear reminder of the terrible financial cost when deterrence fails. The best example of the consequence of losing a high-intensity war fought over one's homeland was the fate that befell Germany in WWII – total destruction of the nation.

UNITED KINGDOM: DEFENCE SPENDING SINCE WORLD WAR II

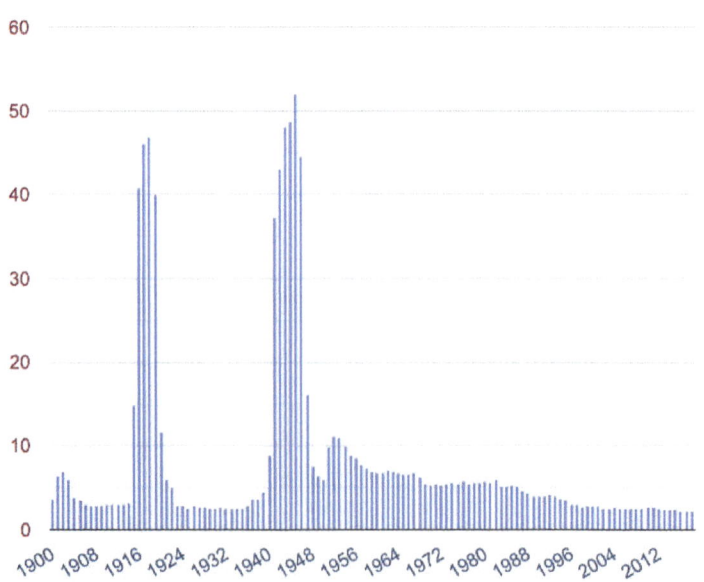

Following WWII, spending remained above 10% for the Korean War. At the peak of the Cold War around the 1970s it was at 5-6%. For the next 25 years, this allowed Britain a sustained and capable level of force projection. Towards the end of the Cold War spending dropped to around 4% as the threat from the USSR steadily receded. Naturally, there was then a peace dividend, as there always has been in Western nations, and average expenditure dropped to around 2%. However, at this lower level of 2%, we have been decreasing our armed forces year after year. As a result, they have been drastically and dangerously weakened. The British government must realise that the time of peace has passed, and that defence spending must be returned to a minimum of 4-5%, levels that were sub-standard during most of the Cold War.

With the long lead times of modern weapons we cannot wait until a war seems imminent or starts. Instead, we must build in higher levels of defence spending and commensurate capability well in advance. Sadly, the geopolitical signals of impending danger are loud and clear.

5.2 FUTURE SPENDING TARGETS

The British people need their politicians and senior military leaders to take action to protect the nation. We need to create a new armed force that acts as a deterrent rather than transmitting the current signal that the West is weak and unprepared. Such a situation historically has only encouraged the next conflict. Most importantly, with the long lead time to build new weapons systems, there will be no chance in a future high-intensity war to recover from the first blow and fight back. We will quite simply live or die as a nation with the capability with which we enter a future war. There will be no second chance. This is a certainty.

To remedy the situation we need to make defence a national priority and radically reorganise our armed forces by increasing spending to 5% of GDP as quickly as possible and adopting a revolutionary new model approach to Britain's Defence.

5.3 UK MILITARY INDUSTRIAL COMPLEX

The great political mistake of the day is to view defence as a cost and not the basis for national growth and expansion through a multiple number of avenues. Increased defence can lead to accelerated design and production techniques. This will both enhance the UK's defence capability and increase the export potential and revenues of her trade. A good example of how this could work is the UK–US partnership in building the F35. This deal amounts to 450 complete F35s which dwarfs the cost of the 148 we have on order. An expanded UK military defence capability can be translated into trade deals and new partnerships that will feed back into the UK and increase GDP and expansion. Defence should not be viewed as a cost, but rather as a catalyst to expand the nation's GDP and global influence. There are strong indications that investment in Defence creates a 2x multiple into the rest of the economy. However, the multiple associated with an economy based on the defence of a global maritime model would be much higher as success of previous maritime empires would attest to.

5.4 CURRENT AND FUTURE SPENDING COMMITMENTS TARGETING 5% OF GDP

With the collapse in GDP to maintain the pre-coronavirus 2%, there will have to be an increase to 3% of GDP just to maintain previous spending levels. This means that to make an effective expansion we are talking about a move to above 5% of the current post-coronavirus GDP levels. However, even with greater spending the need for far greater value for the pound to the taxpayer requires a significant transformation of the defence procurement process.

6.0
THE IMPLEMENTATION PROCESS

6.1 THE NEED FOR A REVOLUTION IN THE MINISTRY OF DEFENCE

The relationship between the MoD and the armed services seems to be deeply flawed and inefficient compared to nations like Japan who operate a larger and more capable defence capability for their metaphorical dollar. The full details of the comparisons between the UK and Japan were detailed in my 2015 Defence Review.

The number one issue we currently face in the MoD is the weaponry acquisition process. In peacetime it is possible to get by with such gross inefficiency in delivery timelines, but in the current accelerating arms' race, extended acquisition times threaten our survival. A revolution must take place at the MoD that creates an Accelerated Defence Procurement Cycle. This is a mechanism whereby the acquisition time is greatly lessened to counter the unfolding revolutions in military affairs that will in the future dominate the effectiveness of the UK's combat forces. The next main blockage is the failure to provide guaranteed full life funding for acquisition programmes. This has been compounded by a stream of constant spending cuts.

6.2 GREATER PROJECT OWNERSHIP

In a UK defence culture where the Four Commands must fight for their budgets, there seems to be a very obvious disconnect and breakdown in responsibility. There is an urgent need for a shift to a culture where the principle is that the team designing and building the weapon system should incorporate the innovative and visionary inputs from the arm that will operate it in combat.

Below: The New Operating Model formalises the relationship between the Commands and Defence Equipment & Support (DE&S). There is now a clearer separation of responsibilities between the Commands, which request equipment, and DE&S, the organisation responsible for buying and supporting the equipment.
© *National Audit Office 2015*

NEW OPERATING MODEL: BUDGETARY FLOW

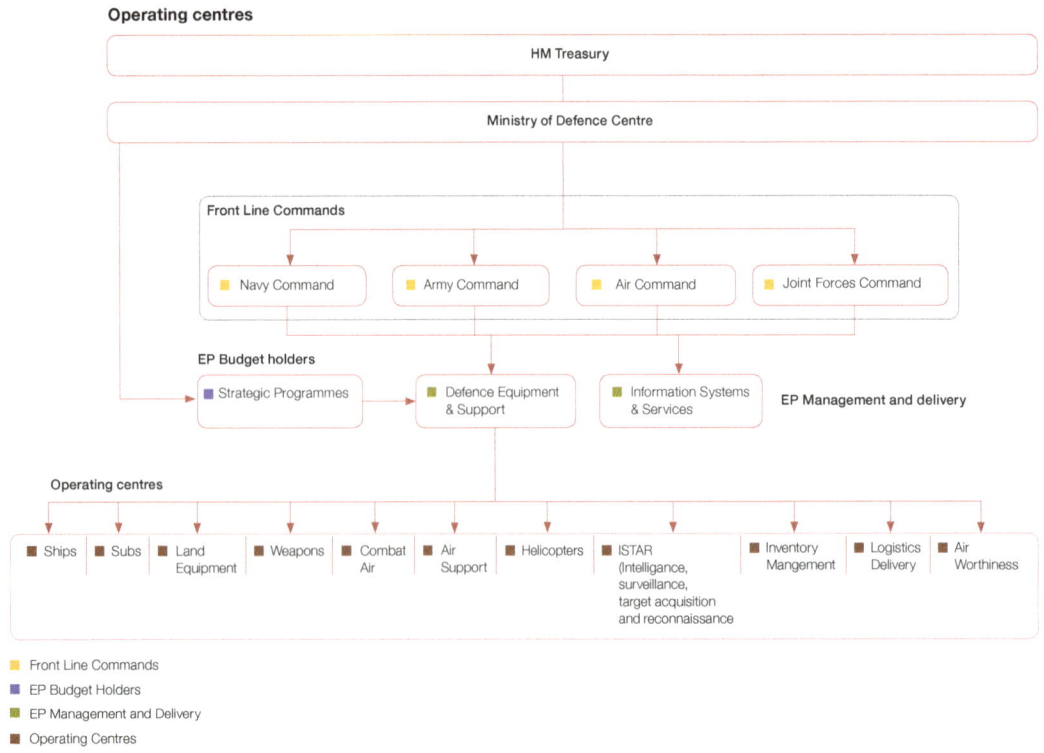

6.3 BUY FROM THE UK OR THE US?

America is building some of the most advanced weapons systems in the world. Where possible and when it is deemed uncompetitive to manufacture, Britain should be buying from the US, with contracts to produce weapons in the UK. However, where there are weapons systems that could be built in the UK at a comparable cost, or when they incorporate new capabilities, they should be.

6.4 THE NEED FOR AN ACCELERATED DEFENCE PROCUREMENT CYCLE

The time between the initiation of a new weapon design to the time it comes into service is far longer than it should be. During this extended timeframe the design shifts to the point where it is a major compromise. Subsequently, it is not fit for purpose. The Ajax specialist vehicle is a clear example of this process, a process that is simply not acceptable.

As we face a time of accelerated RMAs, the rate at which new weapons' systems can be designed and then introduced into service is a war-winning capability. The added advantage of streamlining the procurement process is that with fewer links between those who will use the system and those who design and build it, costs will be reduced and effectiveness enhanced. Taking all of the above information in this article into consideration, I believe the procurement cycle should resemble the following:

1. Development of a tactical battle concept by the relevant command based on an enemy's current and future capabilities. This includes the concept of the weapons systems and force structures required.

2. New design concepts are then opened to a multi-provider design competition. The best designs can be amalgamated into the final design. Key to this process is the use of 3D virtual reality and AI design processes that will dramatically speed up the process and quality of the end product. Companies that invest in this new technology will inevitably have a serious advantage in the design competition.

3. A manufacturing completion then tendered to a manufacturing contract for the fastest and cheapest at a standard quality. As part of this process, the MoD should invest with leading manufacturers in the creation of robotic factories that can be swiftly retooled to build any design within certain box parameters. This later process would create the opportunity for a cost-plus contract system that would be highly efficient for the tax payer.

The creation of such a short design and manufacturing process has massive deterrence and war-winning implications; it could allow a rapid refurbishment of the UK defence capability at a reduced cost. The best example of this in the civilian world is Oracle's win of the America's Cup against New Zealand in 2013, which was ultimately won with a faster design/innovation cycle versus its competition.

6.5 LACK OF AN EFFICIENT INDUSTRIAL COMPLEX

The consequence of a shrinking defence budget has been less spending and a similar shrinkage of the number of defence contractors. The result was a concentration of providers and a reduction in cost-production efficiency that increases the unit costs of each system. Put simply, without sufficient contracting competition for a programme, the costs increase. This vicious negative cycle has been impacting the cost of new weapons systems. This needs to be reversed by bringing in foreign companies who will build UK factories and transfer technology. Despite this contraction, the UK defence sector employs some 130,000 highly skilled people. However, the potential for expansion of the workforce and increased revenues is considerable, when spending is increased. In a time of service economy contraction, the expansion of the UK's military industrial complex has significant potential to stimulate national growth and employment.

Shipbuilding is an good example, and the news that the new RFA support ships will be built in Britain is excellent news. Historically, maritime nations have had core shipbuilding industries, and as such today this should be major government target for economic growth.

6.6 INCREASED SPENDING WILL REDUCE RESEARCH AND DEVELOPMENT COSTS

Britain has managed to keep the basis of a world-class military industrial base that it can now use to expand its national capability. During past decades the cost of research and development (R&D) was spread over a reduced size to the units delivered. The Type-45 is an excellent example. Originally 12 were planned, but only six were delivered. The consequence was that R&D was distributed over fewer ships and unit costs increased. With greater spending this negative cycle should be reversed.

Finding more orders from home and export markets for projects such as the Tempest, as well as new technology developed from the Dreadnought-class SSBN programme provide a few areas of potential focus.

6.7 BETTER EFFICIENCY IN RUNNING LEGACY SYSTEMS

The US defence system is considerably larger than the UK's and as such accessing its companies to provide spare parts for the efficient and cost-effective running of our legacy systems is a key component to future cost savings. Again, competition will reduce costs.

6.8 CONCLUSION

The MoD is the first place that requires evolution, incorporating the above elements, before it is fit for purpose and able to lead dramatic changes to the UK's defence capabilities. This should mean much faster procurement cycles that will inevitably incorporate AI systems and increase automation. However, critical to the success of the procurement process will be the strategic vision regarding weapon systems that will dominate each battle space and subsequently their swift design, manufacture and introduction to operations.

Opposite, top: Type-3 HMS *Northumberland* in the early hours of 30 October 2018 carrying out Naval Gunfire Support (NGS). The Sea Ceptor air defence missile is based on the CAMM series of surface-to-air missiles developed by MBDA for the UK. CAMM shares some common features and components with the air-to-air missile used by the RAF and the surface-to-surface missile to be deployed with the Army. This is an excellent example of the pooling of resources to reduce development costs.
Credit: UK MoD © Crown copyright 2018

Below: A computer-generated concept design of the 'Mothership'. The Royal Navy has unveiled a series of futuristic submarine concepts which mimic real marine lifeforms and radically change the way underwater warfare is fought. The whale shark-/manta ray-shaped Mothership would be built from super-strong alloys and acrylics, with surfaces which can morph in shape. With hybrid algae-electric cruising power and propulsion technologies including tunnel drives which work similarly to a Dyson bladeless fan, the submarine could travel at unprecedented speeds of up to 150 knots. Its 3D-printed hull would be a combination of light but strong acrylic materials bonded to super strong alloys capable of withstanding the extreme pressure of depths of 1,000 metres or more.
Credit: UK MoD © Crown copyright 2019

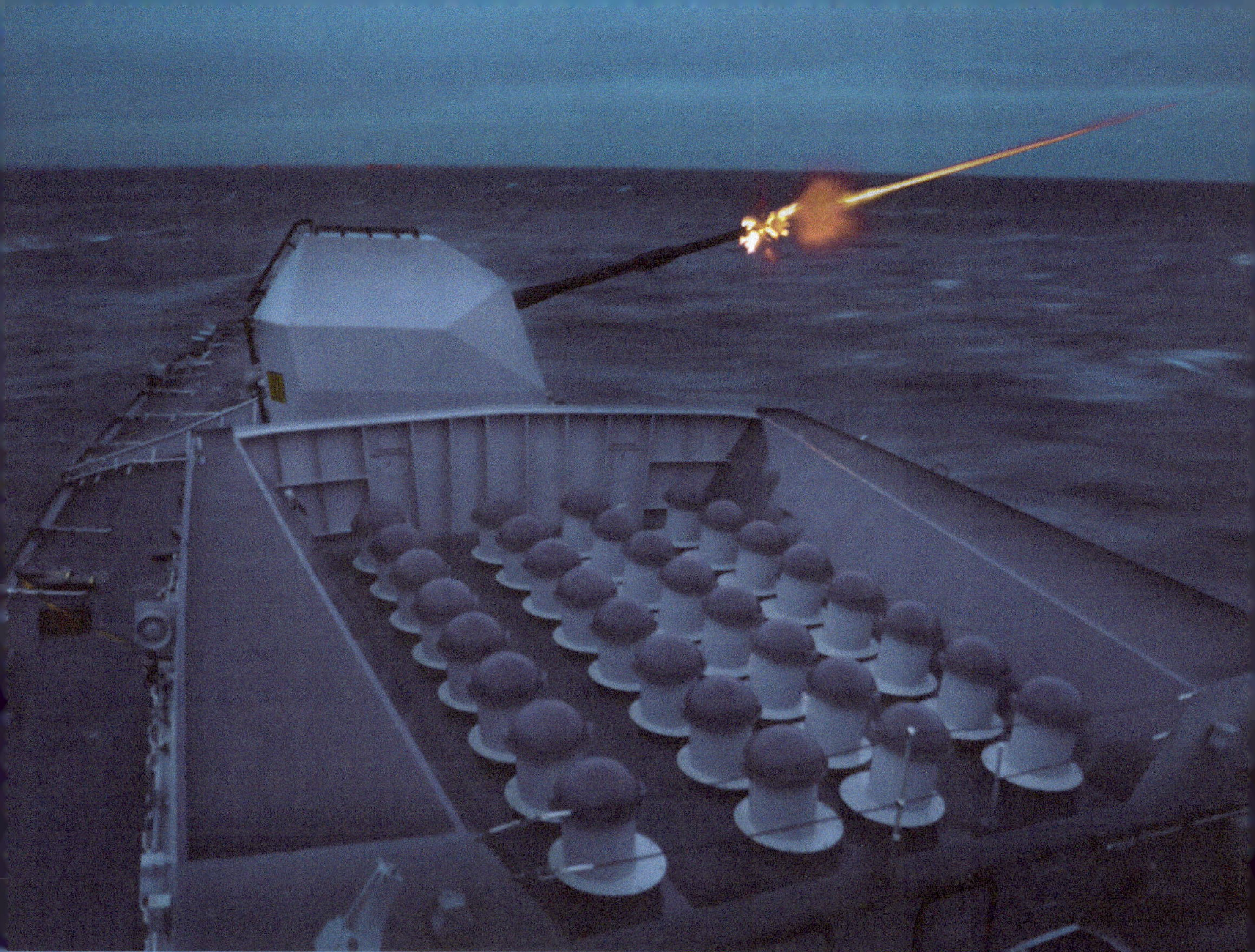
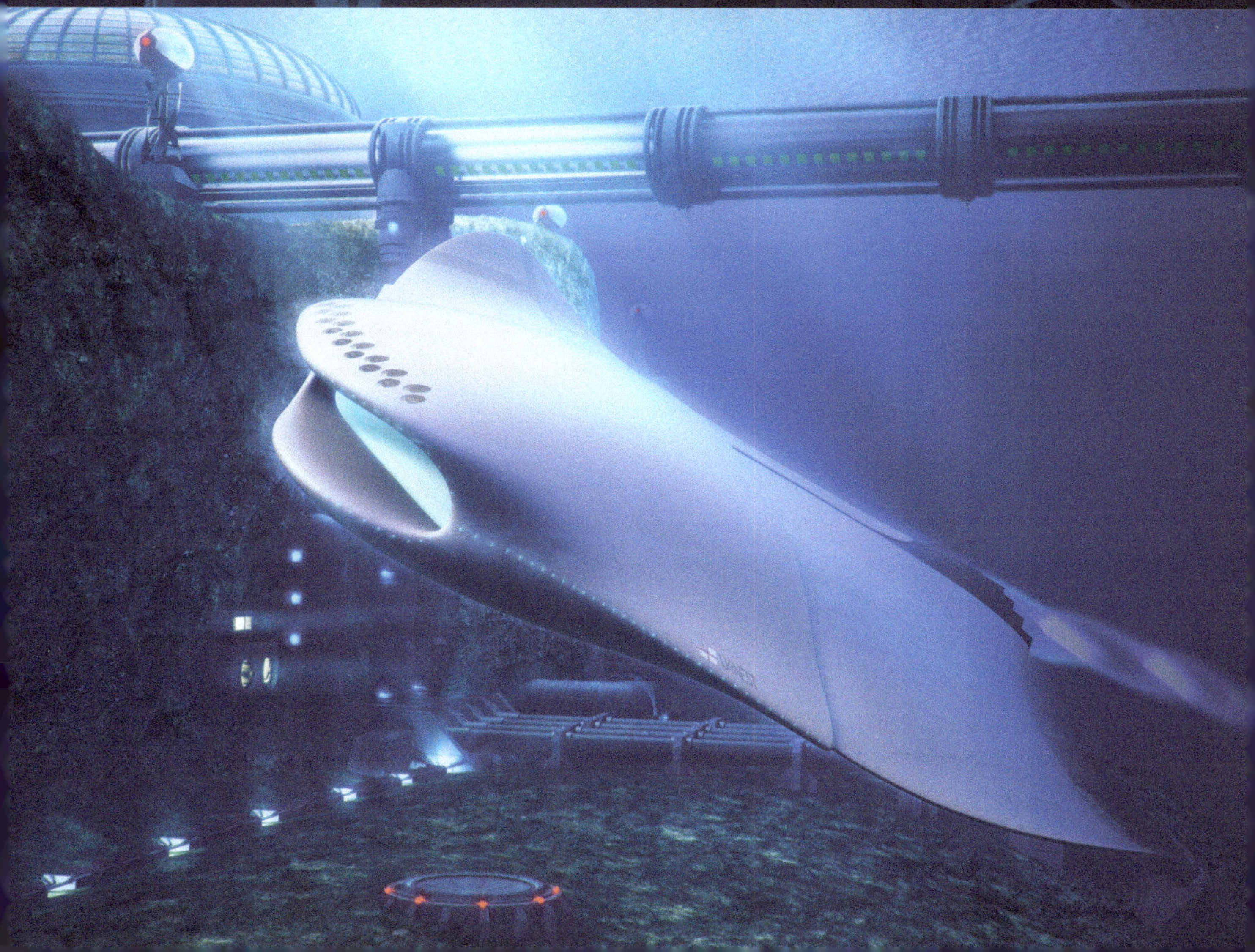

7.0 CONCLUSION: TO BE OR NOT TO BE

7.1 THE KINETIC THREAT TO BRITAIN

The conclusion concerning the decisions about to be taken in this 2020 Strategic Defence Review is that for the fourth time in 110 years, Britain faces an existential threat from Russia, and especially China. A kinetic threat that could by 2025-27 risk the very survival of our nation, if the lamentable condition of our armed forces is allowed to continue. The problem is compounded by multiple revolutions in military affairs that are changing the face of the future battlefield. Thus, it is imperative that this 2020 review both recognises the magnitude of the threat and initiates the rapid expansion of Britain's defence forces. Thus, this is Britain's *Now or Never Moment*, as, due to the long lead times in weapon construction and force optimisation, to be at full strength in five years we need to start right now.

Whilst some leaders in Whitehall might believe that historical analogies are perhaps trite and have no relevance in our modern world, Global Forecaster has proven beyond doubt that once history is decoded into similar sections on the five-phase cycle, historical analogies have very powerful relevance. Whilst the technology of warfare might change and evolve, the nature of human organisations and their repetitive patterns sadly does not.

7.2 THE LESSON FROM OUR HISTORY

As we today face this generation's *Now or Never Moment*, it is appropriate that we return to another such moment that defined Britain and preserved her sovereign status: one that allowed Britain to survive and win the Battle of Britain, 80 years ago in the summer of 1940. Then, Britain faced a battle for its very survival in the skies above Britain, to hold back what was, until then, an invincible and unstoppable force. The magnitude of the victory was perfectly summed up by the immortal words spoken by Churchill, 'that never in the field of human conflict had so much been owed by so many to so few'. But this does beg the question: Who were the few? The obvious answer is that they were the RAF's fighter pilots, of which some 550 gave their lives in the battle. Indeed, they are quite rightly recognised. But lessons from this story tell us of an even smaller number of critical people, who due to their foresight and belief, built the RAF into a machine that was able to resist the German attacks.

7.3 THE EVENT THAT MARKED THE ROAD TO WAR

The story started in March 1936 when Germany marched in to reoccupy the Rhineland without resistance from France. This triggered the almost instantaneous need for rearmament in Britain. The Air Ministry, under huge public pressure to protect the British population from air attack, and against their own judgement that the bomber would always get through, created Fighter Command in May 1936. The invasion of the Rhineland was the signal that Britain faced a *Now or Never Moment* back in 1936. Today that moment was triggered by the annexation of Hong Kong, and as outlined in Appendix VIII, the strategic and geopolitical parallels between China's First Island Chain and Hitler's Siegfried Line and lessons from Hitler's four year plan applied to China today.

Opposite, top: Spitfires of 611 Squadron patrolling over Southern Britain under direction for ground controllers vectoring in on German raiders.
Credit: UK MoD © Crown copyright 1940

Below: WAAF plotters pictured at work in the underground Operations Room at HQ Fighter Command, Bentley Priory, in north-west London. A senior officer studies the unfolding events from the viewing deck above.
Credit: UK MoD © Crown copyright 1940

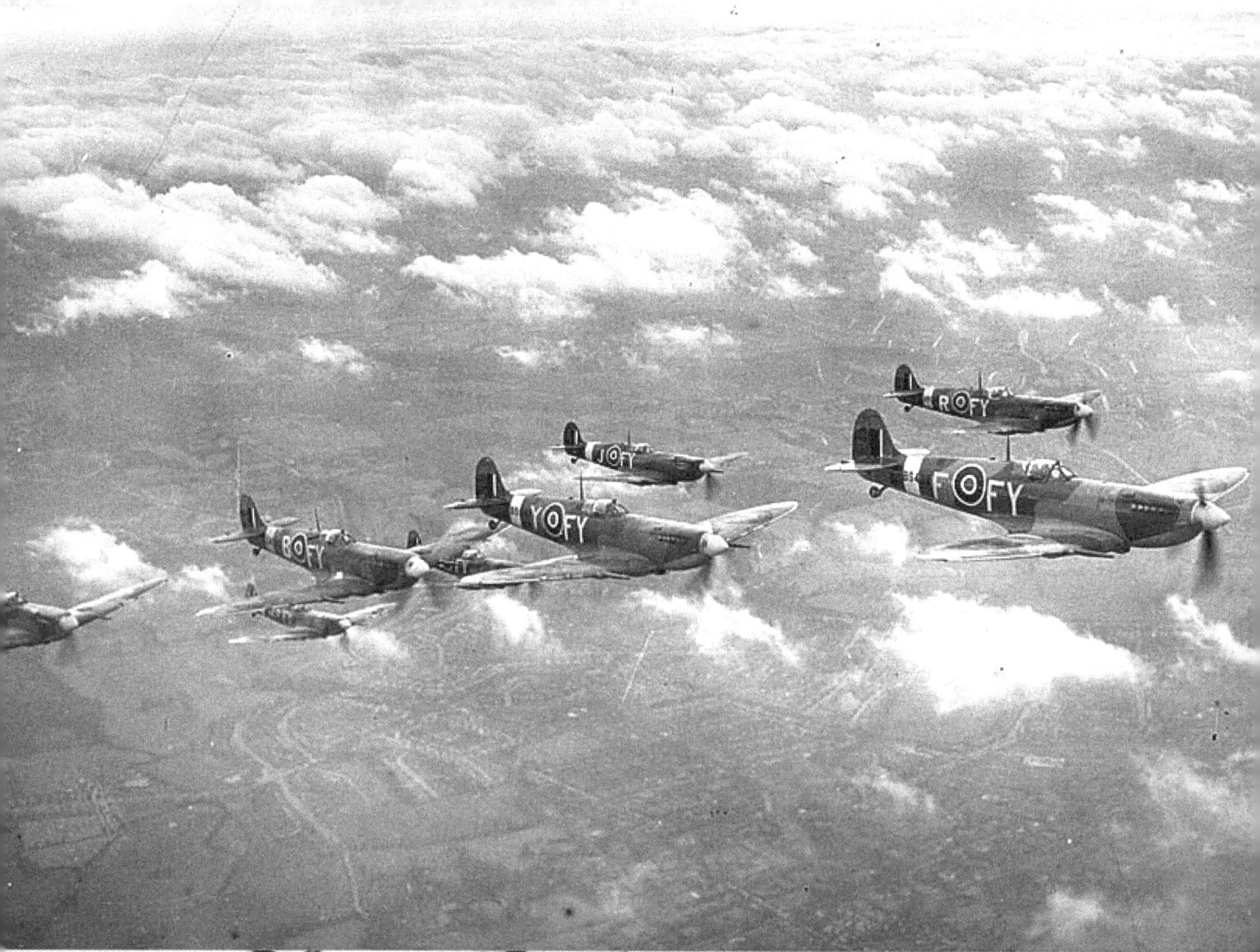

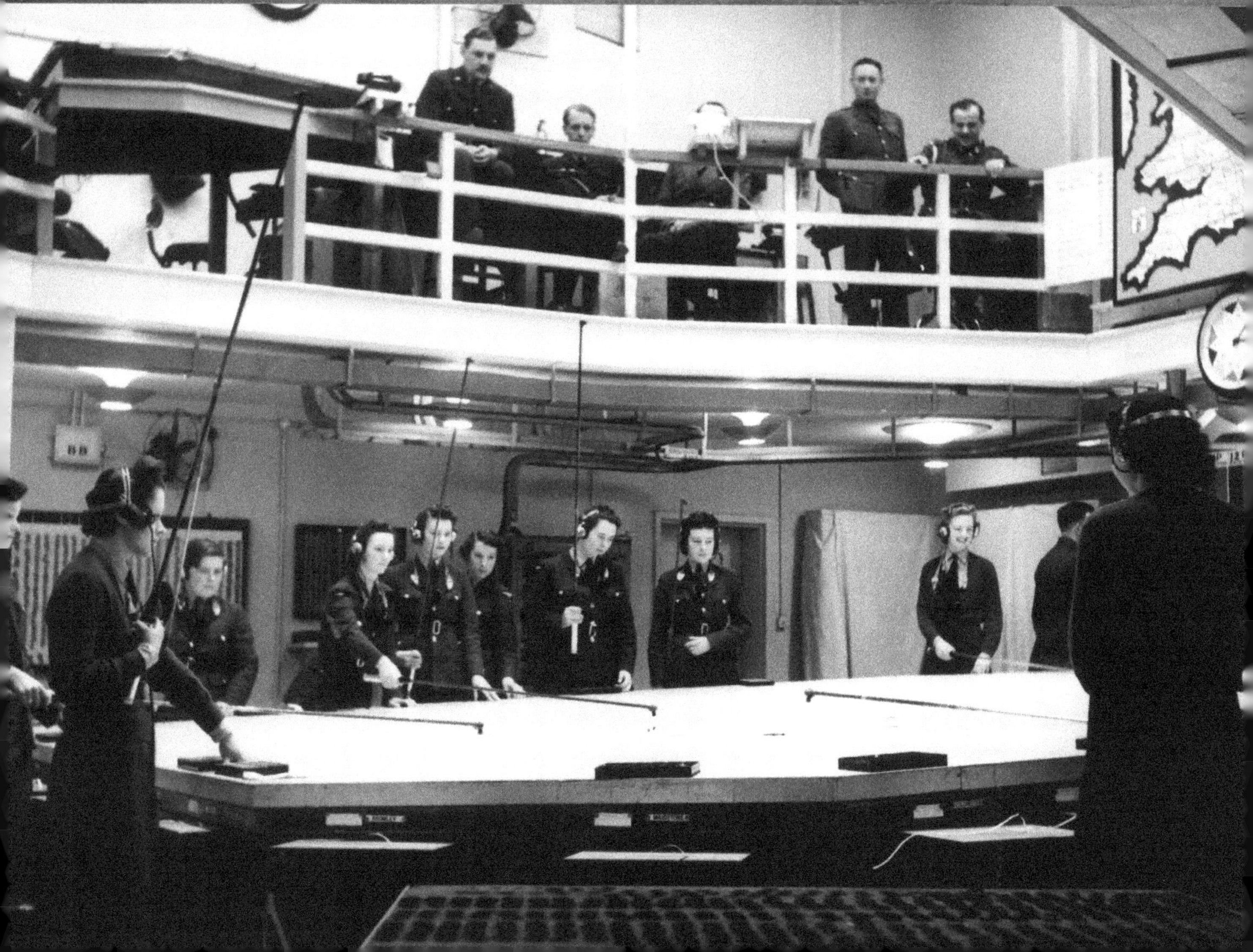

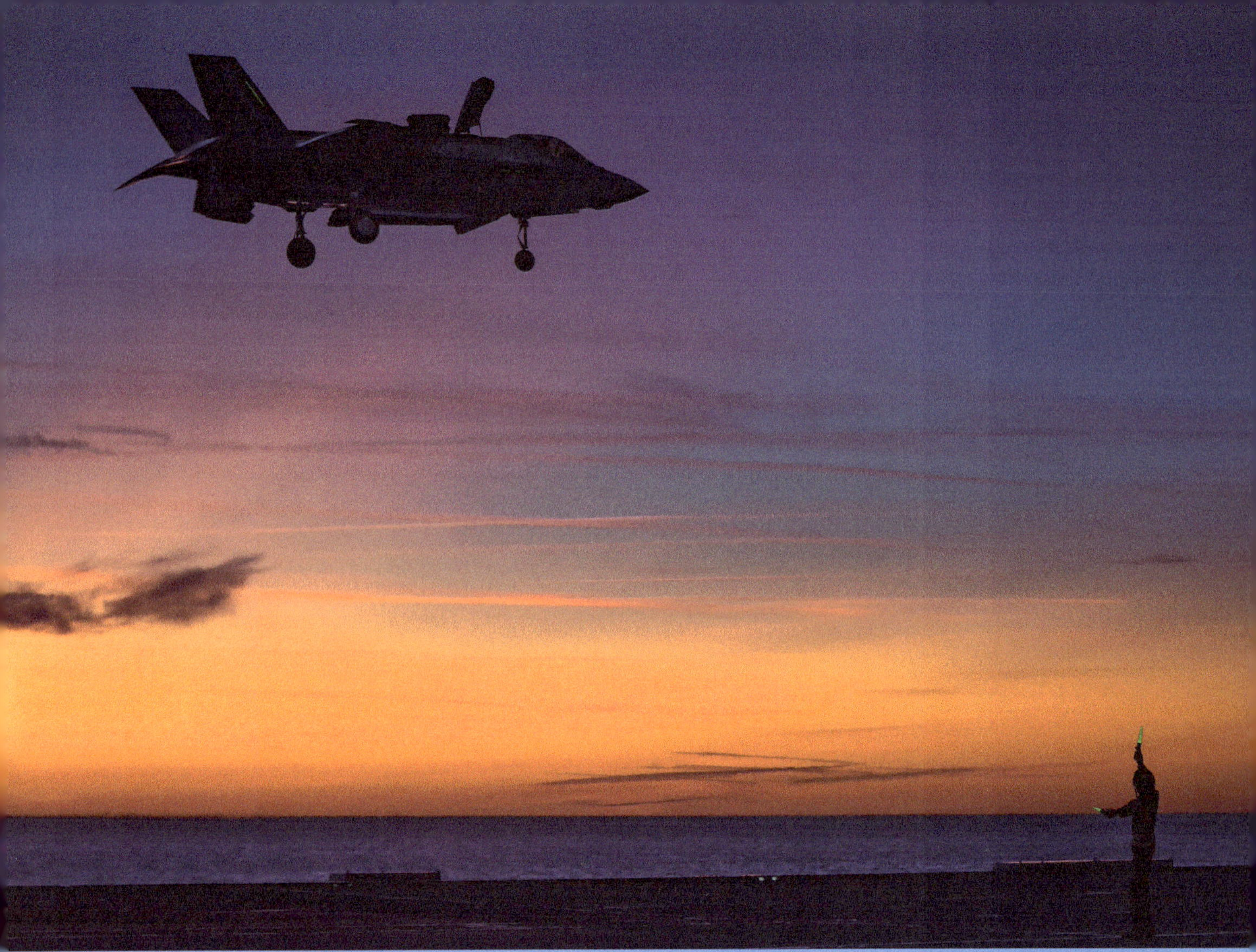

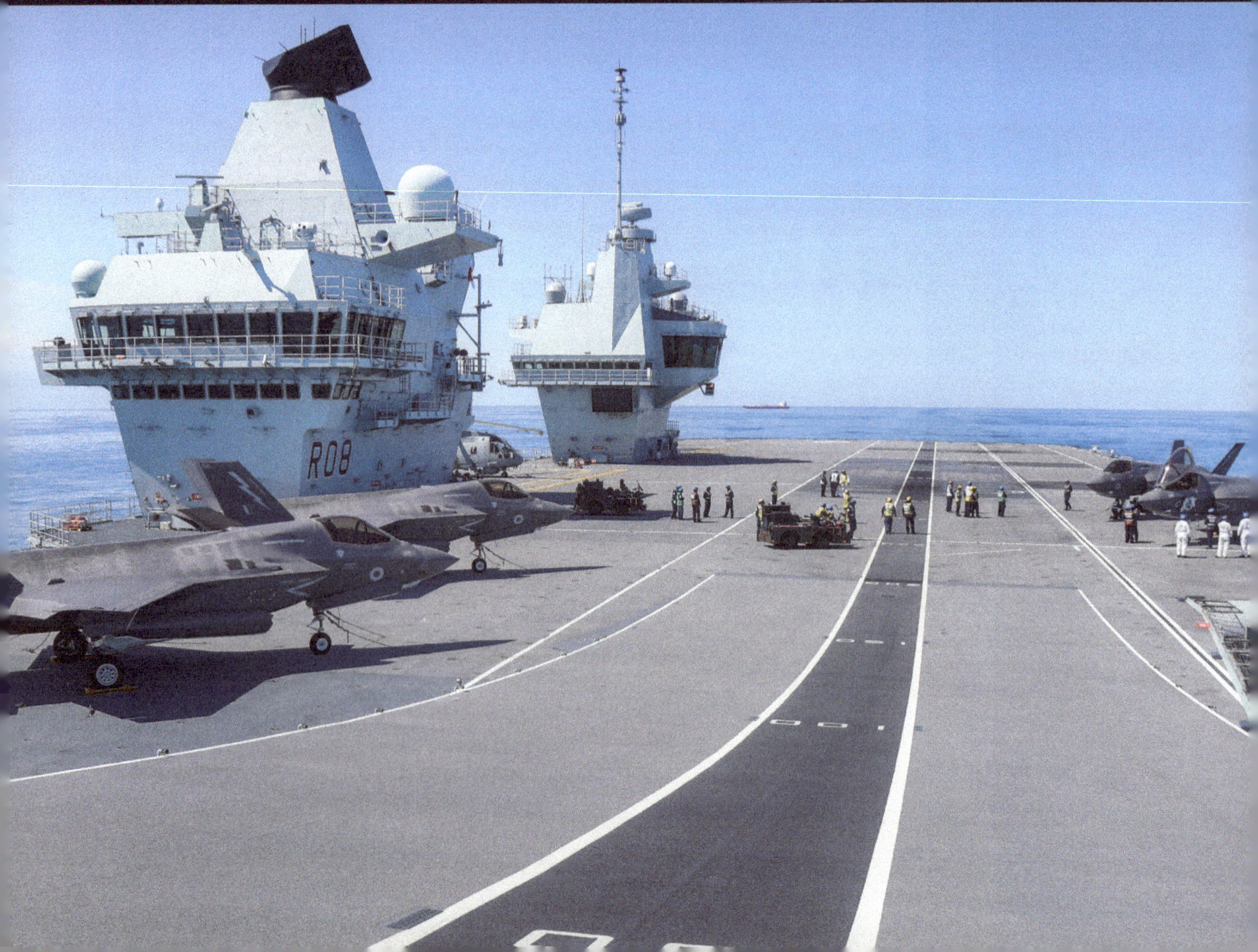
R08

Opposite, top: UK F-35B Lightning fighter Lands on HMS *Queen Elizabeth* during night opps.
Credit: UK MoD © Crown copyright 2019

Below: F-35B Lightning Jets embarked on HMS *Queen Elizabeth* for the first Carrier Sea Training. This marked a new potential dawn for a new post-Brexit maritime Britain. However, to maximise our economic expansion and ensure our national security in these perilous times, we need to increase our investment in Britain's defence and military industrial complex by 150% over current spending.
Credit: UK MoD © Crown copyright 2019

7.4 STRONG VISIONARY POLITICAL LEADERSHIP

German annexation catalysed the first of the few into action, in the form of Winston Churchill, who became increasingly outspoken about the threat that Germany represented, and the inability of the Chamberlain government to meet the growing challenge. Winston warned of Nazi belligerence, saying in the *Daily Mail* that 'a terrible process is astir'.

As such he became the public focus for increased levels of concern, pressuring the complacent Chamberlain government into action and rearmament, and demanding sufficient national funding to do so. Today in Britain there is no politician of similar statue acting in the role of Churchill, but we do have a preponderance of Chamberlain-type energy, denying the obvious threat. Without political leadership to act as a focus for public concern it is impossible to mobilise the nation in its own defence. The only hope is that Boris Johnson and his chief advisor Dominic Cummings become aware of the magnitude of the threat and choose to respond appropriately.

7.5 EXCEPTIONAL MILITARY LEADERSHIP WITH TECHNICAL AND STRATEGIC VISION

Hugh Dowding was appointed as leader of Fighter Command at the moment of its birth. He was a remarkable individual who had fought in the skies of WWI above the Western Front and was the Air Member for Research and Development (1935–36), giving him a unique understanding of new technologies such as radar, and its ability to create the first multi-layered air defence system that would ultimately save Britain. With this vision, he shaped the RAF into a machine that was second to none, and by the summer of 1940, just, and I mean just, it was ready to face the German onslaught. But on top of creating the Fighter Defence System, he also knew how to lead it and fight it, so should be classified as a great wartime commander.

Dowding was the personification of right-brained leadership, who also encouraged similar qualities in his officers. The best example was his exceptional number two, Keith Park, who commanded 11 Group in the Battle of Britain, which controlled the South Eastern Sector, effectively the frontline. Park was a maverick, a gifted war commander and innovative problem-solver, but an individual who the Air Ministry despised. After the Battle of Britain, the Air Ministry sought to diminish him with a sequence of impossible postings, first in command of Fighter Training, where he increased pilot output by multiples, to the chagrin of his superiors, and then to Malta, where they thought he was sure to fail, but instead, he masterminded the defence of the island against impossible odds.

Notably, Dowding was not a politician; in contrast, he was blunt to the point of abrupt when expressing his views up the chain of command. This was a quality that saved his squadrons from being squandered in the battle of France, against Churchill's wishes, which were driven by the political imperative to aid France. For today's armed forces to transform into an integrated force, capable of meeting the future threats, it will require senior leaders of all three main services who all expound the qualities of Dowding. However, the highly politicised military structure of today is such that, in all probability, it has filtered out such qualities as innovative and effective large-scale combat leaders in its senior officers.

7.6 INNOVATION IN WEAPONS DEVELOPMENT

During the Battle of Britain there were 32 squadrons of Hurricanes and 19 squadrons of Spitfires. Whilst the Hurricane was a capable fighter able to take on the bombers, it was not able to outfly the Messerschmitt BF109. Thus, without the Spitfires to take on the BF109 on superior terms, the outcome of the battle would have been very different, as attested by the high victory-to-loss rate of the Spitfire over the Hurricanes. The story of the development of the Spitfire is informative as it was designed by the visionary RJ Mitchell as a short-range interceptor, with an innovative elliptical wing and flush rivets on a light aluminium airframe and skin that give it very high combat speed. However, if it had not been for private funding of the Spitfire's forerunner, the Supermarine S6, to win the Schneider trophy by the patriotic and visionary Lady Lucy Houston, who believed that war was coming, the Spitfire would never have flown. Notably, Spitfire Prototype K 5054 took to the air the day before Hitler marched into the Rhineland on 7 March 1936.

Today, Britain's future weapons need innovative design and innovative funding with accelerated production programmes to bring them into service by 2025.

7.7 THE FINAL ANALYSIS

The sobering thing about the Battle of Britain is what a close run thing it was. Despite all that was done and achieved by RAF Fighter Command. However, without the added combat power provided by the brave and skilled Polish Hurricane 302 and 303 squadrons, who shot down the majority of the 'margin of victory' during the battle, the outcome might have been very different. The most profound observation is that in the final analysis, the battle was lost by the Germans, when, via a directive from Hitler after the bombing of Berlin, the German bombers shifted target from RAF Command's fighter bases, which had been hit to the point of being inoperable, to London. The key lesson, is that if the government had acted more decisively in 1936 to rearm, RAF Fighter Command would have been at a much higher strength level, such that victory in the air over Britain would have been assured, whatever the Germans did.

History is full of examples in which leaders and their governments were distracted by what appeared to be at the time important unfolding events, crises that caused them to fail to respond to a larger magnitude risk that later engulfed them. Today Britain is living though a pandemic that may feel all consuming, but in terms of the magnitude of risk is far lower than that of WWIII. Events such as this global pandemic should be viewed as entropy tsunamis that accelerate trends that are already unfolding, which then forces acceleration in adaptation. Some of those changes will be positive for society, such as increased automation and efficiency of a new emerging economy. Others, such as the accelerated Chinese hegemonic challenge, are much more sinister in their nature and impact.

So, the urgent question for the UK government, as we approach this *Now or Never Moment* in our national defence strategy, is, do we, as a nation, wish to be exposed to the lottery of war through failed deterrence, and chance our survival and victory on the mistakes of our future enemies?

TABLE OF APPENDICES

A full list of the below appendices that are designed to expand on all aspects of *Now or Never: Global Forecaster UK Strategic Defence Review 2020* are available to download at:

https://www.davidmurrin.co.uk/article/now-or-never-the-global-forecaster-2020-strategic-defence-review-appendices

APPENDIX I: GLOBAL FORECASTER WAR THEORY

APPENDIX II: WHEN DETERRENCE FAILS
    Part 1: Third Time Unlucky?
    Part 2: The Politically Forgotten Value of Deterrence
    Part 3: How do the Predatory Presidents Xi and Putin View Britain?

APPENDIX III: SUN ZU'S ART OF WAR APPLIED TO THE CHINESE CHALLENGE TO AMERICA
    Part 1: The Chinese Perspective
    Part 2: The American Perspective
    Part 3: Conflict Management, Deterrence and the Consciousness of a Declining Empire

APPENDIX IV: UK FUTURE WEAPONS DEVELOPMENT
    Part 1: The Brexit Defence Review – The Royal Navy First
    Part 2: The Future of Land Warfare and the Tank

APPENDIX V: THE RUSSIAN THREAT TO THE UK
    Part 1: Intention and Subversion
    Part 2: The Resurgence of Russian Naval Power

APPENDIX VI: THE CHINESE THREAT
    Part 1: The Great Power Shift From West to East
    Part 2: The US-Sino Arms Race; Space And Control of the High Ground

APPENDIX VII: THE LESSON FROM THE HISTORY OF MARITIME HEGEMONY
    Part 1: Lessons from the History of Maritime Hegemonic Challenge
    Part 2: Global Hegemony Requires Shipbuilding to Create a Dominant Navy

APPENDIX VIII: THE LESSONS FROM THE CHALLENGE OF NAZI GERMANY TO CHINA
    Part 1: The Strategic and Geopolitical Parallels Between China's First Island Chain and Hitler's Siegfried Line
    Part 2: Lessons from Hitler's 4 Year Plan Applied to China Today

ABOUT GLOBAL FORECASTER

David Murrin is passionately interested in Defence. As a geophysicist, financier, entrepreneur and historian he is also an expert on both the past and future warfare with a unique perspective on our Armed Forces. He has employed a multi-dimensional approach to assessing our defence capabilities and future imperatives. This has led to *Now or Never: Global Forecaster UK Strategic Defence Review 2020*, which aims to provide an independent assessment of Britain's defence needs at this critical time in our Island history. David invites you to take ownership of our country's future by reading this document and recognising how important Defence will be in preserving our very nation.

Global Forecaster models and predictions are focused on finding deep-seated patterns in history and using them to understand and accurately predict the future in both today's turbulent geopolitical dynamics and financial markets. These predictions are based on David's book *Breaking the Code of History*, which uses a series of unique models to describe human systems and their cyclical behaviour that are applicable to empires, nations, military organisations and companies. One of the core models is the five-stage roadmap which has had a remarkable track record of predicting events over the past two decades. Details of the models and predictions can be found at **www.globalforecaster.co.uk**

One of the first Global Forecaster predictions in 2003 was that the war against Islamic fundamentalism was not the main threat to Britain and the West. But rather it was rise of China and its hegemonic challenge to America, i.e. the onset of strategic competition, trade wars and a new arms race in the decades ahead that would come to a dangerous head in 2025–27 with the risk of WW3. Almost 17 years later that prediction is looking frighteningly accurate.

www.globalforecaster.co.uk

www.davidmurrin.co.uk/breaking-the-code-of-history

ALSO BY THE SAME AUTHOR

BREAKING THE CODE OF HISTORY (2009)
This book outlined many prescient predictions, which have proved frighteningly accurate. David predicted that climate change was both real and that its effects would accelerate faster than any predictions at that time. He predicted the decline of America, and the exponential rise of the hegemonic challenge of China, with its associated accelerating arms' race that by 2025 would lead to a very high risk of World War III. David also predicted in 2007 that the next global pandemic would be a virus that originated from a Chinese weapons factory.
www.davidmurrin.co.uk/breaking-the-code-of-history

LIONS LED BY LIONS (2018)
This book exposes the greatest divergence between a story told and its reality – that of the British Expeditionary Force (BEF) during World War I. The book outlines the mistakes by British politicians that led to the outbreak of the war, including their failure to invest in full-spectrum deterrence and expound the commensurate political intention. Today we are making those very same mistakes with China. Critically, *Lions Led by Lions* repudiates the perception of lions led by donkeys and explains that the lions of the BEF were actually led by lions within a technologically advanced British army that won the war.
www.davidmurrin.co.uk/book/lions-led-by-lions

RED LIGHTNING – HOW THE WEST LOST WORLD WAR III TO CHINA IN 2025 (2021)
Since the end of the Cold War the majority of the populations of the West have lived with the assumption that World War III (WWIII) would and could never take place. However, what if an aggressive and expansive hegemonic challenger believed that the combination of the West's collapse in collective moral fibre and resolve, coupled with the use of powerful and decisive new weapons deployed en masse, could make WWIII winnable? This is the story of how the past ten years and next five years comprise the road to war in 2025 and the moment that China mounts surprise attacks on the free world. Red Lightning then precisely details how the PLAN wins WW3 in only a few days and ends the rule of democracy globally.
https://www.davidmurrin.co.uk/book/red-lightning

Lightning Source UK Ltd.
Milton Keynes UK
UKHW050613210223
417371UK00007B/105